Excel

ADVANCED SKILLS

ENGLISH YEAR 2 AGES 7–8

# GRAMMAR AND PUNCTUATION WORKBOOK

Get the Results You Want!

PASCAL PRESS

Donna Gibbs

Reprinted 2014, 2016 (twice), 2018, 2020, 2021, 2022

ISBN 978 1 74125 442 6

Pascal Press
PO Box 250
Glebe NSW 2037
(02) 8585 4050
www.pascalpress.com.au

Publisher: Vivienne Joannou
Project editor: Mark Dixon
Edited by Leanne Howard
Reviewed by Dale Little and Kristine Brown
Cover and page design by DiZign Pty Ltd
Typeset by lj Design (Julianne Billington)
Printed by Vivar Printing/Green Giant Press

# Contents

# To the student

*This book explains the rules of grammar and punctuation that you need for Year 2.*

*Each unit focuses on two or more grammar rules. Before each rule is explained, there is a text that lets you see how the rule works in everyday writing. These texts are important as they are models of the different text types and will help you in your own writing. At the end of each unit there is also a short NAPLAN-style test that lets you see how well you have understood the grammar rules.*

*Most of the activities can be written in this book, but you will have to use your own paper for the writing activity at the end of each unit. I suggest you buy a notebook or folder for this. The writing activities are very important. The more you do, the faster your English will improve. If you are not sure how to write something, use the example texts as a model.*

*It is important that you work through this book from Unit 1 to the end. This will help you build your skills and become a more confident speaker and writer of English. Make sure that you understand the work in each unit before you go on to the next one. Remember to have a dictionary handy as you work through the book, and to ask for help if you need it. There is a glossary on page 85 that explains the grammatical terms used in the units.*

*I hope you enjoy reading the texts and doing all the activities.*

*Good luck!*

*Donna Gibbs*

# About this book

This book consists of fourteen units, each covering one or more aspects of grammar or punctuation. Each unit is theme-based and contains two texts designed to introduce the grammatical features and to show students how they function in context. These are followed by detailed explanations of how and why the grammar features are used, as well as exercises that allow students to put the knowledge they have acquired into practice. As an aid to revision, there is a glossary at the end of the book that summarises the grammatical terms used in the units.

The exercises in the units are organised as follows:

### Let's find them!

- These exercises require students to find examples of the grammatical feature in question in the texts. They are straightforward exercises designed to test recall.

### Let's go to the next step!

- This set of exercises is more difficult, requiring students to apply the knowledge they have acquired.

### Let's aim high now!

- These are challenging exercises, again requiring students to apply what they have learnt.

### Let's put it all together now!

- This is an editing exercise designed to test the students' understanding of the material covered in the whole unit. It also acts as a revision exercise.

### Let's have fun!

- Although this exercise is designed to be fun, it is also challenging. It reinforces the material learnt.

### Let's have a test!

- This series of eight NAPLAN-style questions helps students revise for the NAPLAN Tests and also tests their knowledge of the material learnt in the unit as a whole. The questions are graded so that they increase in difficulty.

### Let's write now!

- This activity encourages students to write their own text in which they use the grammar and punctuation they have learnt in the unit. The texts are based on the theme and text types featured in the unit.

Most of the exercises in this book consist of six questions, as we believe they give students the practice they need to fully grasp the rules of grammar and punctuation.

# Unit 1 Wild animals

*Common nouns*

## My safari

My **family** and I went to the zoo at the weekend. Many of the animals were out on a vast, grassy **plain** just like in the wild in Africa.

First, we spent time at the bird hide, looking at the birds. Then later in the morning we went on a safari. We sat in a **jeep**. It took forty minutes to drive around. The tallest animals we saw were giraffes. We also saw a family of zebras snoozing in the sun. We saw some rhinos and hippos as well. It was so much fun.

In the afternoon we went on a walking trail. We saw **lions**, meerkats, more hippos, some cheetahs and the gorillas.

The gorillas were my favourite animals of the day.

*by Jenny*

This is a **recount**. A recount tells about things that have already happened. Jenny uses **common nouns** to name people, places, animals and things seen at the zoo.

**Common nouns** name people, animals, places, and things; for example, **family** (people), **lions** (animals), **plain** (places) and **jeep** (things).

## Let's find them!

Find the **common nouns** in the text which name the following.

For example: the time of day before lunchtime ______morning______

1. a kind of motor vehicle ______________________
2. the tallest animals seen by the family ______________________
3. animals that were snoozing in the sun ______________________
4. a path made for walking on ______________________
5. animals that Jenny saw in two different places ______________________
6. Jenny's favourite animals ______________________

## Let's go to the next step!

Choose a **common noun** from the box to match each group below. The first one has been done for you.

> **Tip!** You may need to use your dictionary for help with some of the questions.

| | | | |
|---|---|---|---|
| plains | cockatoo | kangaroo | jaguar |
| evening | doctor | walrus | |

1. lion, tiger, cheetah, jaguar
2. wallaby, wombat, dingo, ______
3. rivers, forests, parks, ______
4. kookaburra, magpie, lorikeet, ______
5. police officer, truck driver, zookeeper, ______
6. seal, otter, polar bear, ______
7. dawn, dusk, morning, ______

## Let's aim high now!

Sort the **common nouns** from the box into the correct column. The first row has been done for you.

| | | | | |
|---|---|---|---|---|
| vet | hippos | bats | cheetahs | forests |
| gorillas | driver | rivers | grassland | zoos |
| food | leopards | parks | doctor | tails |
| visitor | waterholes | bus | family | lions |
| trees | ticket | map | meerkats | |
| plains | zookeeper | hats | cleaner | |

| People | Animals | Places | Things |
|---|---|---|---|
| vet | gorillas | plains | food |
| | | | |
| | | | |
| | | | |
| | | | |
| | | | |
| | | | |

## Mountain gorillas

Mountain **gorillas** live in **forests**. They eat **bark**, stems, leaves, flowers and fruit from plants. Their main food is bamboo. They do not drink water very often. They get water from the plants they eat.

Gorillas live in family groups called troops. They make nests. Their daytime nests are for resting in the day. These are simple nests on the ground. Gorillas also build night nests. These are built in trees.

Gorillas have long arms. They mostly walk on their knuckles. They can walk on two feet for a short distance. They have a big head and no tail.

The mountain gorilla is an endangered species in the wild. **People** around the world are working to save the gorilla from extinction.

This is an **information report** about mountain gorillas. Information reports give factual information about things. **Common nouns** are used to name where the gorilla lives, what it eats and how it looks.

**Common nouns** name people, animals, places and things; for example, **people**, **gorillas**, **forests** and **bark**.

# Let's find them!

Find the **common nouns** in the text that complete these sentences.
For example: Mountain gorillas live in ______forests______.

1. The main food mountain gorillas eat is ____________________.
2. Gorillas rarely drink ____________________.
3. Gorillas build ____________________ for a resting place.
4. Night nests are built in ____________________.
5. Gorillas mostly walk using their ____________________.
6. Gorillas can walk short distances on two ____________________.

## Let's go to the next step!

Choose a **noun** from the box to complete each sentence. The first one has been done for you.

| species | troop | nests | heads | plants | forests | tails |
|---|---|---|---|---|---|---|

1. Gorillas eat plants.
2. Gorillas are an endangered ______.
3. Gorillas live in ______.
4. Gorillas build two kinds of ______.
5. A group of gorillas is called a ______.
6. Gorillas do not have ______.
7. Gorillas have big ______.

## Let's aim high now!

Circle the animal **noun** in each list of common nouns.
For example: zoo, elephant, jeep

1. seed, flower, lion
2. kangaroo, nest, tree
3. forest, hippo, savannah
4. enclosure, fence, giraffe
5. trail, tiger, track
6. monkey, mountain, moat

# Let's put it together now!

Circle the **common nouns** in the text below. You should find fifteen of them. The first one has been done for you.

There are gorillas at the zoo who live on an island. They have huge chests and very long arms. The father has silver fur on his back. He has bright, intelligent eyes. He can hold a stick in his toes. When the mother wants the children or their father, she claps her hands.

# Let's have fun!

Create a safari trail map in the space below.

1. Add an entrance, waterhole, kiosk, lookout and exit. Add labels to your drawings.
2. Draw a trail that starts at the entrance, wanders through the park and ends at the exit.
3. Choose five different kinds of animals to place in your safari park. Draw and label them as you add them to your map.

# Let's have a test!

In questions 1–2, which noun completes the sentence?

1 Gorillas are ____________________.

- ◯ zoos
- ◯ animals
- ◯ plants
- ◯ mountains

2 A jeep is a ____________________.

- ◯ bus
- ◯ helicopter
- ◯ train
- ◯ vehicle

In questions 3–4, which word is the noun in the sentence?

3 I saw some gorillas playing.

- ◯ I
- ◯ saw
- ◯ some
- ◯ gorillas

4 Giraffes are very tall.

- ◯ Giraffes
- ◯ very
- ◯ are
- ◯ tall

5 Which of these words is a noun?

- ◯ happy
- ◯ bird
- ◯ hungry
- ◯ thirsty

6 Choose the noun that names a person.

- ◯ fence
- ◯ flower
- ◯ zookeeper
- ◯ jeep

7 Choose the noun that names a place.

- ◯ lion
- ◯ gorilla
- ◯ zoo
- ◯ monkey

8 Choose the noun that names a thing.

- ◯ rhino
- ◯ snake
- ◯ children
- ◯ nest

**Tip!**
Shade the circle next to the correct answer.

# Let's write now!

Write an **information report** about the animal you would most like to see on an animal safari. You may need to look up your choice of animal to find out more about it. Use **common nouns** to tell about where the animal lives, what it eats and how it looks.

# Unit 2 People and places

*Proper nouns; capital letters*

## Our trip to Kangaroo Island

My mum, dad and I, and the **Grahams** from next door, went for a trip to **Kangaroo Island** in January. We drove there in our old Holden. We had to leave our dog, Rusty, behind.

We put our car on a ferry called the *Sealion 2000* at Cape Jervis. My dad drove the car off the ferry at Penneshaw and we had arrived! Kylie Minogue was on our ferry but mum and dad told us not to stare.

We all wore our Aussie bush hats called Akubras. On our walks we saw seals and beehives and lots of wildflowers. There were gum trees growing along the creeks and rivers. I saw a koala asleep in a very tall **Blue Gum**.

It was the best trip ever and I'd really like to go again.

*by Trent*

This is another **recount**. Trent uses **proper nouns** to name particular people, animals, places and things in telling about his trip.

**Proper nouns** name particular people, places, animals and things; for example, **Grahams** (people), **Kangaroo Island** (places), **Rusty** (animals) and **Blue Gum** (things).

## Let's find them!

**Tip!** **Proper nouns** can have more than one word in their name; for example, **Kangaroo Island**.

Find the **proper nouns** in the text which name the following.
For example: the family from next door ___Grahams___

1. a brand of car ____________________
2. a ferry ____________________
3. the place the family got off the ferry ____________________
4. a famous singer ____________________
5. a brand of bush hat ____________________
6. a species of tree ____________________

## Let's go to the next step!

Choose a **proper noun** from the box to match each group. The first one has been done for you.

| | | | |
|---|---|---|---|
| Donald Bradman | Melbourne | Sally | James |
| Maritime Museum | Mrs Wong | Ford | |

1. Sydney, Hobart, Adelaide, Melbourne
2. Cathy Freeman, Samantha Stosur, Ian Thorpe, ________
3. Tom, Koba, Liam, ________
4. Auntie Mary, Uncle Bill, Mr Wong, ________
5. Nicky, Amanda, Anna, ________
6. Australian Museum, British Museum, Powerhouse Museum, ________
7. Toyota, Mazda, Holden, ________

## Let's aim high now!

Choose **proper nouns** from the box to complete these sentences. The first one has been done for you.

| | | | |
|---|---|---|---|
| November | Tuesday | Koala-Lou | Luna Park |
| Australia | Greece | Olympic Games | |

1. I have a soccer game after school on Tuesday.
2. My birthday is in ________.
3. She won a gold medal at the ________.
4. Did you see the koala named ________ in the tree?
5. Our family loves visiting ________.
6. Canberra is the capital city of ________.
7. My Greek grandfather came to Australia from ________.

## A good dream

I had a good dream last night. I went on a world tour with my friend **Koba**.

Our first stop was to see some statues in **China**. I'd seen pictures of them on television. They were statues of warriors who were buried in front of the tomb of Emperor Qin Shi Huang.

Our next stop was Mount Fuji in Japan. I have seen pictures of it in a book. In my dream, Koba and I climbed to the top and peeped into the crater. I don't know if that would happen in real life!

Our last stop was at Disneyland Park in America. We floated to all the different lands: Tomorrowland, Fantasyland and Adventureland. Koba talked to Indiana Jones at Adventureland but I was too shy!

*by Sophie*

This is another **recount**. Sophie writes proper nouns with **capital letters** to name people and places in her dream.

Proper nouns always have **capital letters**; for example, **Koba**, **China**.

# Let's find them!

Find the **proper nouns** in the text that name the following.

For example: Sophie's friend Koba

1. a ruler of China in the past ______________________

2. a mountain ______________________

3. the country where you can see Mount Fuji ______________________

4. an entertainment park ______________________

5. three imaginary lands ______________________

   ______________________ ______________________

6. a character from film and television ______________________

## Let's go to the next step!

The **proper nouns** in the text below have lost their capital letters. Circle them and write them correctly. The first one has been done for you.

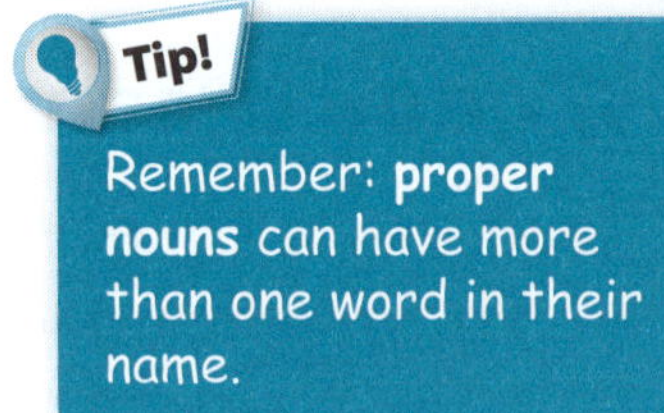


On wednesday, 3rd april this year we went to disneyland. There were well known figures such as mickey mouse and donald duck. I liked travelling in tomorrowland the best.

1. Wednesday
2. ____________
3. ____________
4. ____________
5. ____________
6. ____________

## Let's aim high now!

Some of the words in these boxes should **not** have capital letters as they are not proper nouns. Cross them out, leaving only **proper nouns** in the boxes.

| People I'd like to meet | Things I'd like to eat | Places I'd like to go |
|---|---|---|
| Father Christmas | Chocolates | Darwin |
| Sister | Vegemite | River |
| Anthony Browne | Anzac Biscuits | Island |
| Great-Grandfather | Apples | Tasmania |

# Let's have fun!

1 Using your atlas to help if necessary, add these place names to the map of Australia.

New South Wales
Victoria
Tasmania
South Australia
Western Australia
Northern Territory
Queensland
Australian Capital Territory (ACT)
Pacific Ocean
Indian Ocean

2 Think of three people who live or have lived in Australia. Add their names, and the place where they lived, to the map.

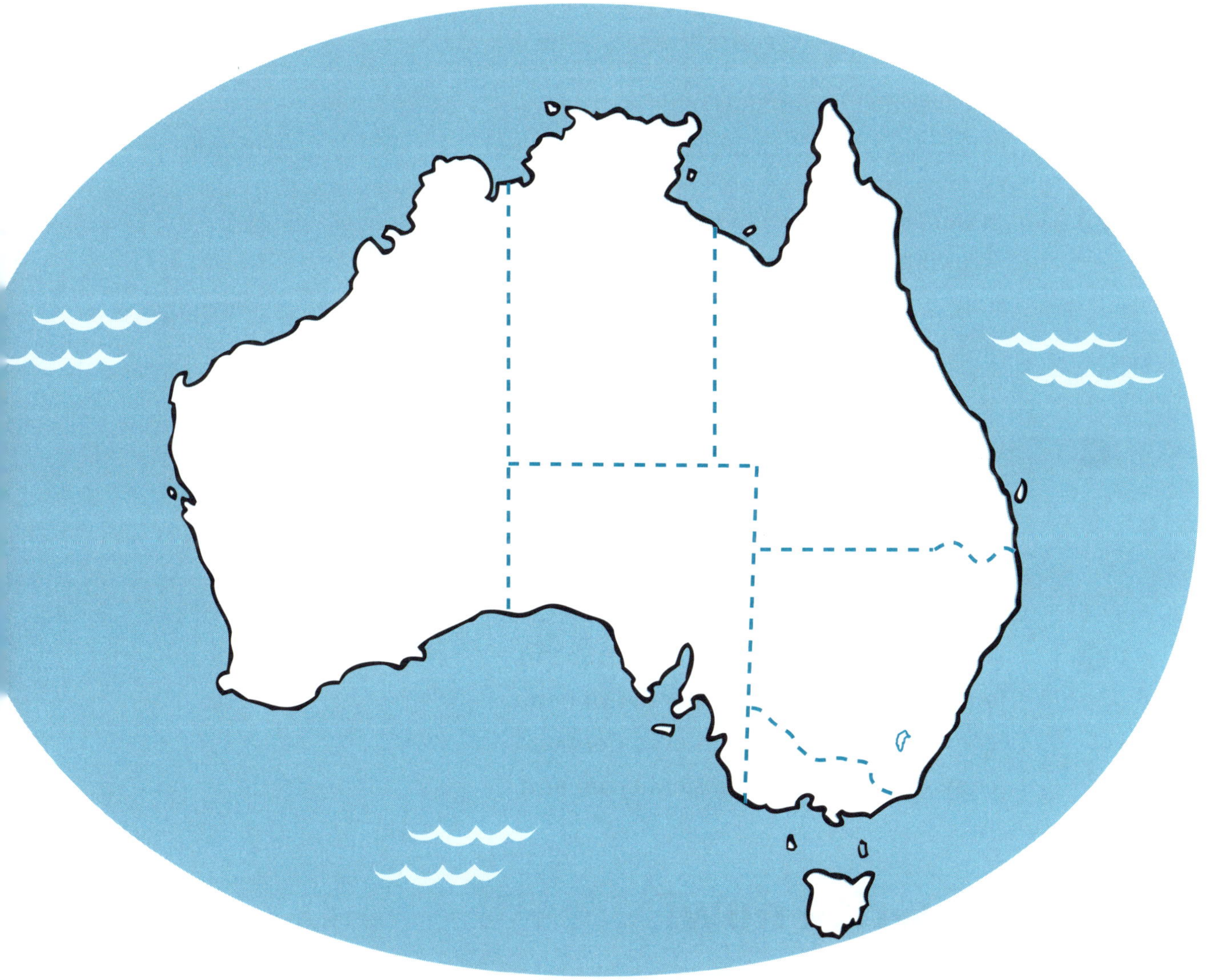

# Let's have a test!

In questions 1–3, which word is a proper noun in the sentence?

1. My dog, Rufus, has a very loud bark.
   - ◯ dog ◯ Rufus ◯ loud ◯ bark

2. Her mum drove her to school in their Toyota yesterday.
   - ◯ Toyota ◯ school ◯ mum ◯ yesterday

3. My birthday is on the 7th November and we are having a party.
   - ◯ My ◯ birthday ◯ November ◯ party

In questions 4–5, which word has lost a capital letter?

4. Are you going to visit canberra soon?
   - ◯ you ◯ going ◯ canberra ◯ soon

5. Dr Begg lives nearby and has a red mazda.
   - ◯ lives ◯ nearby ◯ red ◯ mazda

6. Which word should **not** have a capital letter in this sentence?
   Sally Brown had Toast and Vegemite for breakfast.
   - ◯ Sally ◯ Brown ◯ Toast ◯ Vegemite

In questions 7–8, which sentence uses capital letters correctly?

7. ◯ You can see indiana jones at adventureland.
   ◯ You can see Indiana jones at Adventureland.
   ◯ You can see Indiana Jones at adventureland.
   ◯ You can see Indiana Jones at Adventureland.

8. ◯ Jenny saw the prime minister in canberra.
   ◯ Jenny saw the Prime minister in Canberra.
   ◯ Jenny saw the Prime Minister in Canberra.
   ◯ Jenny saw the Prime minister in canberra

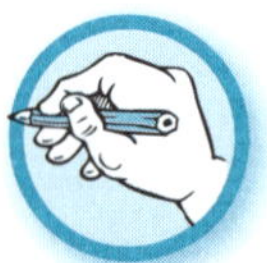

# Let's write now!

Write a **recount** about places you have visited in Australia. Remember to use a **capital letter** for particular names of people, animals, places and things.

Adjectives

# Unit 3 At the beach

## The beach in autumn

Our **long**, **hot** summer is over. It is autumn and there are colder days now. I watch the glassy, greenish waves dash into the shore. They leave patterns of lacy water behind them on the **wet** sands. A **chilly** wind is blowing. Look! The wind has caught a huge umbrella and is tossing it around as though it were an old toy. The dark, cloudy sky makes it seem as if rain will fall soon.

I am sitting on our picnic rug in my green swimming costume. I have tiny goose bumps all over my arms and legs. I'm too cold to get into the rough, swirling water. Now my striped beach towel is wrapping itself around my shivering legs. Brrr. I wish I was at home in front of a cosy, hot fire.

This is a **description**. A description helps us to form pictures in our mind of people, places and things. This description uses **adjectives** with **nouns** to describe what the beach looked and felt like in autumn.

**Adjectives** are words that describe nouns; for example, a **long**, **hot** summer; **wet** sands; a **chilly** wind.

## Let's find them!

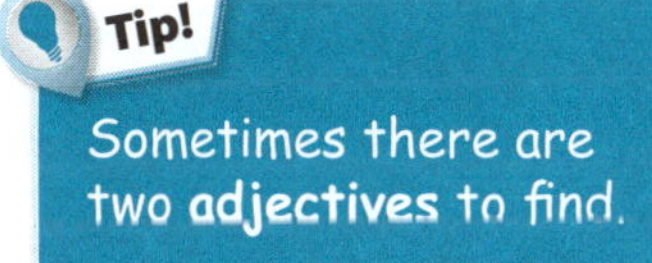


Find the **adjectives** in the text that describe the following.
For example: the autumn days ____colder____

1. how the waves look __________ __________
2. how the water looks __________
3. the size of the umbrella __________
4. the colour of the swimming costume __________
5. the size of the goose bumps __________
6. the fire __________ __________

## Let's go to the next step!

Choose an **adjective** from the box to match each group. The first one has been done for you.

| | | | |
|---|---|---|---|
| cool | sour | fantastic | hot |
| yellow | huge | little | |

1. crunchy, tasty, sweet, ______sour______
2. tiny, small, mini, ____________
3. big, large, gigantic, ____________
4. wonderful, marvellous, beautiful, ____________
5. warm, heated, scorching, ____________
6. cold, freezing, icy, ____________
7. blue, red, green, ____________

## Let's aim high now!

Choose an **adjective** from the box to complete each sentence. The first one has been done for you.

| | | | |
|---|---|---|---|
| three | plastic | naughty | chilly |
| giant | jagged | third | |

1. A ______chilly______ wind was blowing up cold sea spray.
2. There were only ____________ fish left in the rock pool.
3. I got ____________ place in the swimming race.
4. That looks like a ____________ stingray to me.
5. I can see two children playing with ____________ buckets and spades.
6. The sea was crashing against the ____________ rocks.
7. Did you see the ____________ seagull swoop down and pinch my chips?

## The beach in summer

Summer holidays are here again. The **many beautiful** beaches of sunny Queensland are waiting for you and your family! There are **long** stretches of **white** sand. Tall palm trees wave a welcome in the gentle breezes. Calm, blue waters lap lazily into the shores.

You might catch sight of a friendly pelican or some pretty little shells. You can build a giant-sized sandcastle or snorkel in the deep waters. There are fascinating rock pools to explore. When you tire of being on the beach you can visit a café for a delicious ice-cream or a juicy mango.

There are two things to do right now. Pack your bags and travel to sunny Queensland. You'll have the holiday of a lifetime.

This is an **advertisement**. Advertisements persuade people to do things. This advertisement uses **adjectives** to give information about Queensland in order to persuade people to go there for a holiday.

**Adjectives** give different kinds of information about the nouns they describe; for example, number (**many**), opinion (**beautiful**), size (**long**) or colour (**white**).

# Let's find them!

Find the **adjectives** in the text that describe the following.

For example: the colour of the waters that lap the shores ____blue____

1. the size of the shells ____________________
2. the size of the sandcastle ____________________
3. the author's opinion about the pelicans ____________________
4. the author's opinion about the rock pools ____________________
5. the author's opinion about how the ice-cream tastes ____________________
6. the number of things to be done ____________________

# Let's go to the next step!

Mary is making a list of reasons to persuade her parents to take her to the beach. Her adjectives are not good choices for this purpose. Help her by replacing the **adjectives** that are bolded with ones from the box. The first one has been done for you.

| | | | |
|---|---|---|---|
| blue | sunny | 365 | fishing |
| fantastic | good | salty | clear |

1. In summer, there are lots of **miserable** days. sunny
2. I practise my swimming in the **dirty**, **black** water at the beach.
   ______ ______
3. There is a **rotten** sandcastle competition each year. ______
4. You can feed the seagulls **700** days a year at the beach! ______
5. I love the **foul** smell of sea air. ______
6. You can catch fish easily with a **clothes** line from the rocks. ______
7. Swimming is very **bad** for my health and fitness. ______

# Let's aim high now!

Sort the **adjectives** from the box into the correct columns. The first set has been done for you.

| | | | | | | |
|---|---|---|---|---|---|---|
| beautiful | six | tiny | little | gigantic | fantastic | most |
| long | ugly | bright | rosy | eighty | last | pretty |
| blue | first | another | amazing | dark | red | cream |
| small | funny | wonderful | greenish | huge | mini | few |

| Number | Size | Colour | Opinion |
|---|---|---|---|
| six | long | blue | beautiful |
| | | | |
| | | | |
| | | | |
| | | | |
| | | | |
| | | | |

# Let's put it together now!

Circle the **adjectives** in the text below. You should find fifteen of them.

Our holiday house has thirty steps down to the beach. On warm, sunny days I pack my old swimsuit, my favourite, striped towel, sandwiches and a cold drink into my bag. Then I run down the steps and find a good spot on the warm sand.

Sometimes I like to build a huge sandcastle on our beach. My biggest sandcastle had four levels and a wide moat. It was the best sandcastle I've ever made.

# Let's have fun!

Draw and colour in a beach scene which has the following:

1. a lifesaver in a red swimsuit
2. a lifesaver in a blue swimsuit
3. two flags
4. a flying seagull
5. a tiny crab
6. yellow sand
7. fluffy clouds
8. a small boy
9. a tall girl in a big sunhat
10. a striped towel and a spotted beach bag

# Let's have a test!

In questions 1–2, which adjective completes this sentence correctly?

1 When it is a ______________________________ day we love to go swimming.

- ◯ funny
- ◯ creepy
- ◯ sunny
- ◯ wicked

2 I can dive off the diving board at the ______________________________ end now.

- ◯ heavy
- ◯ soft
- ◯ full
- ◯ deep

In questions 3–4, which adjective adds information about number?

3
- ◯ few
- ◯ pink
- ◯ cloudy
- ◯ smooth

4
- ◯ cold
- ◯ sunny
- ◯ eight
- ◯ long

In questions 5–6, which adjective adds information about size?

5
- ◯ round
- ◯ oval
- ◯ orange
- ◯ gigantic

6
- ◯ blue
- ◯ naughty
- ◯ short
- ◯ rough

In questions 7–8, which adjective offers information that is an opinion?

7
- ◯ each
- ◯ wonderful
- ◯ red
- ◯ long

8
- ◯ pretty
- ◯ striped
- ◯ green
- ◯ sunburnt

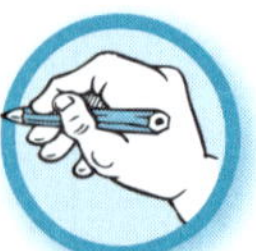

# Let's write now!

Imagine you are looking at a beach scene through some binoculars. Write a **description** of what you see. Use **adjectives** to show what is in the scene and how it looks.

# Unit 4 My class

**Focus**
*Full stops; commas*

## Lochie's Diary

6th March

Dear Diary,
I started in Year Two today. There are 28 children in my class. My class is called Two Green.
The teacher asked me to sit next to Eva Miller. Eva gave me a big smile. She helped me put my things away. I think we will become friends.
Our teacher is called Ms Blewett. She seems friendly and I like the work she has given us so far. We did some Maths. Then we did some handwriting. Best of all was the drawing lesson we had. She helped us to draw the face of the person next to us. I drew Eva and she drew me.
At the end of the year, the whole of Year Two is going on a camp. I can't wait.

This is a **diary entry**. A diary entry is a personal record written in date order. Lochie uses **sentences** ending with **full stops** to make pauses between sentences in his record of events on 6th March.

**Full stops** make a pause between sentences. A full stop is the dot at the end of a sentence that tells you it is complete; for example, **I started in Year Two today.**

## Let's find them!

Find the sentences from the text ending in a **full stop** that give the following information. The first one has been done for you.

1. the name of Lochie's class ________ My class is called Two Green.
2. who Lochie sits beside ________
3. what Eva did to help Lochie ________

4 Lochie's teacher's name ______________________________

______________________________

5 what Lochie and Eva drew ______________________________

______________________________

6 how much Lochie wants to go on the Year Two camp ______________________________

______________________________

## Let's go to the next step!

When Lochie wrote this diary entry he forgot to use any full stops. Add seven **full stops** to complete his sentences. The first one has been done for you.

It is time for our camp at last. We leave tomorrow at 7 am I have packed

my sleeping bag and some warm clothes I've got some chocolate milk and

fruit scones for morning tea I hope I can sit next to Bill on the bus

We are going to swim and rock climb It should be really good

## Let's aim high now!

There are seven missing **full stops** and seven missing **capital letters** in the sentences below. Add them in the correct places. The first one has been done for you.

1 Eva sits next to me. ~~she~~ **She** is good at maths.

2 Mike had a new lunchbox it had stickers on the lid.

3 Ms Blewett is our teacher she has two children of her own.

4 I like our new classroom do you like it?

5 Eva likes ballet her sister does too.

6 Our new tables are yellow yellow is a happy colour.

7 I did a painting it is a picture of Eva.

## The Year Two camp

At last, it was time to set off. We were going to our first camp. The driver put our **sleeping bags, cases and boxes of food** in the bus. Two hours later, we arrived at Lake Myong.

I got very sleepy on the bus trip. As we got near, everyone started singing, chanting and calling out. That woke me up, thank goodness!

After we arrived, it was time to put up our tents. I unpacked my sleeping bag, pyjamas, toothbrush and toothpaste. Once that was done, it was time for fun. We had bats, balls and skipping ropes to play with. In the evening, we learned some magic tricks. After that, we had a camp fire.

For breakfast the next day, we had toast, sausages and eggs. I played rounders, mini-golf, tennis and cricket. In my view, camps are great fun.

*by Dotti*

This is another **recount**. Dotti uses **commas** to separate items in lists as she tells what happened at the Year Two camp.

**Commas** make a short pause between words. They are used to separate words in a list; for example, **sleeping bags, cases and boxes of food**.

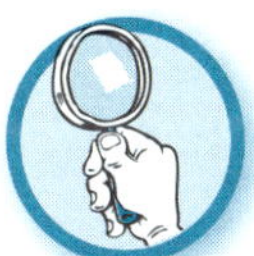

# Let's find them!

Tip!

You don't usually need a **comma** before the last *and* in a list.

Find words separated by a **comma** in the text that list the following. The first one has been done for you.

1. things the driver put in the bus sleeping bags, cases and boxes of food
2. kinds of noise made as they got near Lake Myong ______________________
3. things Dotti unpacked ______________________
4. things they had to play with ______________________
5. what they ate for breakfast ______________________
6. games the children played ______________________

# Let's go to the next step!

The lists in these sentences have lost their **commas**. Add them where they are needed. The first one has been done for you.

1. Mr Quick packed cases, backpacks and boxes of food.
2. We needed paper pencils and cards to play the game.
3. Would you pass me my t-shirt book and sweets?
4. They played rugby soccer and cricket at the camp.
5. The magician found a rabbit a coin and a feather in my ear!
6. You have to take a sleeping bag pyjamas and a wash bag to camp.
7. We had pears ice-cream and jelly for dessert.

# Let's aim high now!

Add a **comma** to make a pause before the space. Then add an item from the box to the lists in the sentences below. The first one has been done for you.

| | | | |
|---|---|---|---|
| danced | dry | jeans | ice-cream |
| white | books | t-ball | |

1. You can choose from tennis, t-ball and basketball.
2. Our school colours are green ______________ and dark blue.
3. We had strawberries ______________ and chocolate topping.
4. There were games ______________ and CDs at the camp.
5. We sang ______________ and made music.
6. I wore a jumper ______________ and sneakers at camp.
7. Our tents kept us warm ______________ and cosy.

# Let's put it together now!

Ms Rosewood has listed twenty items to buy before she goes to camp, but her shopping list is hard to read. Write them in categories to help her organise her shopping, putting **commas** between each item.

| | | | |
|---|---|---|---|
| bandaids | tomato sauce | bananas | watermelon |
| lamb chops | toilet rolls | cheese | sausages |
| raisin bread | lettuce | bread rolls | eggs |
| bandages | tomatoes | Vegemite | sliced bread |
| shampoo | minced steak | milk | apples |

Bakery: ________________________________________

Bathroom items: ____________________________________

Fruit and vegetables: ________________________________

Groceries: ________________________________________

Meat: __________________________________________

# Let's have fun!

Sometimes, adding a **comma** changes what a sentence means. The sentences in the boxes below have exactly the same words but different punctuation. Draw a picture in each box to show you understand what the sentences mean.

| | |
|---|---|
| **1a.** Eva has some chocolate milk and fruit for morning tea. | **1b.** Eva has some chocolate, milk and fruit for morning tea. |
| **2a.** Lochie is putting his orange, drink bottle and beach towel in his bag. | **2b.** Lochie is putting his orange drink bottle and beach towel in his bag. |

# Let's have a test!

In questions 1–2, which punctuation mark makes the sentence correct?

1. It is fun in my new class

○ ,  ○ ?  ○ !  ○ .

2. We caught a bus to the camp

○ ,  ○ ?  ○ !  ○ .

3. Where should the full stop go to separate these two sentences?

Everyone had to put ○ up their ○ tents ○ Afterwards, they ○ ate dinner.

In questions 4–8, show where the comma should be.

4. We ate ○ our dinner ○ lit the camp fire ○ and sang ○ some songs.

5. We took ○ off ○ our hats ○ raincoats ○ and gumboots.

6. The teacher told us ○ to bring ○ pencils ○ books ○ and our lunch.

7. She wanted to bring ○ her pillow ○ teddy and ○ duvet ○ to the camp.

8. She got out ○ her bag ○ uniform ○ and socks ○ for the next day.

# Let's write now!

Write a **recount** about your first day in a new class or your first class camp. When you have finished, check that you have used **commas** and **full stops** correctly.

# Unit 5 At school

**Focus**

*Question marks; exclamation marks*

## Sam's first day

"Good morning. Welcome to Year Two. My name is Ms Raye. **What is your name?**"

"My name is Sam Seldon, Ms Raye."

"Sam is a new student. What do you say, Year Two?"

"Good morning, Sam."

"How old are you, Sam?"

"I'm seven, Ms Raye."

"You'll be in Olley house. What sports do you like?"

"I like cricket and Aussie Rules. We had Aussie Rules in Melbourne. Do you have Aussie Rules here in Sydney?"

"Yes we do, Sam. The team here is called the Sydney Swans. Have you heard of them?"

"Yes, Ms Raye. Where should I put my bag?"

"Will you show Sam the lockers please, Jenny? He can have the locker next to yours."

This is a **conversation**. Conversations are spoken exchanges between people. This conversation has been written down. **Question marks** are used when Ms Raye or Sam ask a question.

A **question mark** is placed at the end of a sentence that asks a question; for example, **What is your name?**

## Let's find them!

Find the **question** in the text that asks the following.

For example: what Year Two should say "What do you say, Year Two?"

1. what Sam's age is ____________________
2. what sports Sam likes ____________________
3. what Sam asks about Aussie Rules ____________________

____________________

4 what the teacher asks Sam about the Sydney Swans ______________________________

______________________________________________________

5 what Sam asks about his bag ______________________________

## Let's go to the next step!

Some of the sentences below need a **question mark** and some need a **full stop**. Add the correct punctuation mark to the sentences. The first one has been done for you.

1 Are you coming home with me today (?)

2 Did you paint that picture ( )

3 I play in the under-8 team ( )

4 They are going to a new school next term ( )

5 Are we there yet ( )

6 Am I taking my new lunchbox to school today ( )

7 I am starting at my new school tomorrow ( )

## Let's aim high now!

Number the answers so that they match up with their **questions**. The first one has been done for you.

| Questions | Answers |
|---|---|
| 1 When does Ali start school? | 1 Ali is starting school today. |
| 2 When will you get a new teacher? | Ms Raye lost her old briefcase. |
| 3 Why did Ms Raye get a new briefcase? | Lunchtime begins at 12.30. |
| 4 When does lunchtime begin? | We have choir after school. |
| 5 When do you go camping? | No. My school uniform is far too big for me. |
| 6 When do you have choir? | Our first camp is in Year Three. |
| 7 Does your school uniform fit you well? | Next year we will have a new teacher. |

## The best swimming carnival ever

This year our swimming carnival was the best swimming carnival we have ever had. **Wow! It was so exciting!**

When the carnival was nearly over each of the houses had one hundred points. We were all level!

I was in the last race swimming for Preston house. The swimmers in Olley house were ahead. Then the swimmers for Whiteley got a bit ahead of them. Then it was the second-last lap and I swam as hard as I could. Preston was in the lead! Could we keep it up?

The last swimmers were neck and neck. The judges said it was almost a dead heat! Who won? It was Preston! Hooray! Now can you understand why I said our swimming carnival was fantastic?

*by Kelly*

This is another **recount**. Kelly uses **exclamation marks** to add to feelings of excitement in telling about what happened at the swimming carnival.

Exclamations express strong feelings such as pleasure, surprise, anger and disgust. They end with an **exclamation mark (!)**. An exclamation mark can be placed after a single word (e.g. **Wow!**) or at the end of a sentence (e.g. **It was so exciting!**).

# Let's find them!

Find the **exclamation** in the text that expresses the following.

For example: the houses had level scores _____ We were all level! _____

1. who was in the lead _____
2. what the judges said _____

_____
3. who won the carnival _____
4. how excited Kelly felt _____

## Let's go to the next step!

The sentences below need an **exclamation mark** and/or a **full stop** to be complete.
Add the correct punctuation.
For example: We won the swimming carnival. Hooray for us!

1. Harry walks to school each day
2. It is fifteen kilometres to Harry's school He walks there and back every day
3. The school canteen sells salad, rolls and fruit for our lunches
4. I can have a sleepover Yippee
5. That's horrible Yuk
6. Our school play this year is *Mary Poppins*

## Let's aim high now!

Choose the correct **punctuation mark** from the box to complete the sentences below.
The first one has been done for you.

| ! | ! | ! | ? | ? | ? | . |
|---|---|---|---|---|---|---|

1. That's disgusting (!)
2. Did you enjoy the swimming carnival ( )
3. Oh wow, our school play is the best ( )
4. I made my own lunch today as the canteen was closed ( )
5. Did you watch the relay ( )
6. What time does school finish ( )
7. Ouch, that hurt ( )

# Let's put it together now!

Tina uses too many **exclamation marks** in her writing. Circle seven exclamation marks you could take out of her text and replace them with **full stops**. The first one has been done for you.

I am starting at my new school tomorrow (!). Lizzy who lives next door has said I can walk with her to school! She will show me where everything is! She said she would introduce me to her friends as well! I have a new schoolbag and a new uniform to wear tomorrow! It is green! I've also got new white socks and a new lunch box! But even so, I'm scared stiff!

*by Tina*

# Let's have fun!

Two children, who sit next to each other at school, have just met. Write a **conversation** between them as they walk home together. Include three **questions** and two **exclamations**. Write your questions in green, your exclamations in red and any other sentences in blue.

# Let's have a test!

1. Which sentence is a question?
   - ◯ What time does school start?
   - ◯ School starts at 9 am.
   - ◯ School has started already!
   - ◯ The bell rings when school starts.

In questions 2–3, which sentence needs a question mark?

2. - ◯ Football practice is today.
   - ◯ We have football practice on Thursdays.
   - ◯ I missed football practice today.
   - ◯ Is there football practice today.

3. - ◯ Our school is very old.
   - ◯ How old is your school.
   - ◯ Your school is almost new.
   - ◯ I think our school is over one 100 years old.

4. Which sentence is an exclamation?
   - ◯ Will you help me?
   - ◯ Help!
   - ◯ He helped her when she fell over.
   - ◯ I hope you will help me carry my bag.

In questions 5–6, which punctuation mark should end the sentences?

5. Why didn't you go to school yesterday
   - ◯ ?
   - ◯ .
   - ◯ !
   - ◯ ,

6. Hooray for holidays
   - ◯ ?
   - ◯ .
   - ◯ !
   - ◯ ,

In questions 7–8, which sentence needs an exclamation mark?

7. - ◯ She put her rubbish in the bin.
   - ◯ The children picked up their rubbish.
   - ◯ The teacher put her rubbish in the bin.
   - ◯ The rubbish bins look disgusting.

8. - ◯ We learned that caterpillars turn into butterflies.
   - ◯ What a disaster.
   - ◯ We are studying space in science this term.
   - ◯ I am going to visit our sister school next year.

**Tip!**

It is very easy to overuse **exclamation marks** so be careful not to use too many in your writing.

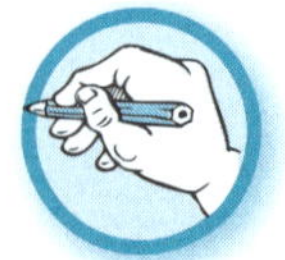

# Let's write now!

Write the **conversation** between two people having lunch together in the playground or at a sporting carnival. Take care to use **question marks** and **exclamation marks** when they are needed.

# Unit 6 Neighbours

**Personal pronouns; singular and plural**

## The family next door

10th January

Dear Diary
Yesterday my **family** was asked next door for afternoon tea. **We** had not met the Coopers as they had only just moved in. Mr and Mrs Cooper have three children called Anna, Mark and Jake. They seem very nice.
The grown-ups drank tea and there were scones for them. The children had fruit juice and cakes. I had a blueberry muffin and it was yummy.
After tea, my brother and I were told we could go outside to play with the Cooper children. We climbed some trees and played hopscotch. I asked them if they would be coming to our school now. Mark said he thought they were starting there on Monday.
Anna wants to walk to school with me. I think she might become a new friend.
by Molly

This is another **diary entry**. Molly uses **personal pronouns** in her diary entry in the place of **nouns** already mentioned. This saves her having to repeat the nouns.

**Personal pronouns** are words that are used in the place of nouns; for example, **we** stands for **family**. Pronouns are used to save repeating nouns.

## Let's find them!

Find the **personal pronouns** in the text which stand for the following.

For example: the word *Coopers* ____they____

1. the word *children* ____________
2. the word *grownups* ____________
3. the word *muffin* ____________
4. the words *my brother and I* ____________

**Tip!**
The personal pronouns are: **I, me, you, he, him, she, her, it, we, us, you, they, them.**

5 the word *Mark* ______________

6 the word *Anna* ______________

## Let's go to the next step!

Choose the correct **personal pronoun** to complete these sentences.
For example: My name is Molly and ____I____ was invited to visit next door.

1 My sister is going out as ______________ has been asked to afternoon tea.

2 I sat on the chair then pushed ______________ nearer to the table.

3 Anna and I played hopscotch then ______________ climbed a tree.

4 Mr Cooper was hungry and ______________ ate four scones.

5 Anna likes our school and ______________ thinks it is a happy place.

6 Mark has brown hair and ______________ is curly.

## Let's aim high now!

The underlined personal pronouns are used to stand for nouns that have already been mentioned. Write the **pronoun** and the **noun** it stands for on the lines below.
For example: Give me the plate as it needs to be put on the table. ____it, plate____

1 Jim invited a friend over to his house. ______________

2 Anna gave Molly another muffin although she had already eaten two.

______________

3 The Coopers have invited us for dinner and they said to come early.

______________

4 Do you think Susan will wear the dress her mother gave her this afternoon?

______________

5 I want Jake to come to our house as it is a really good place to play.

______________

6 "Hello, Anna. Are you going to walk to school with me today?"

______________

## My friends from next door

**I** have three good friends called Anna, Mark and Jake. **They** are our neighbours. Anna is tall and has brown hair. She wears it in a ponytail. She also likes to play hopscotch. It is her favourite game just now. We walk to school together as it is not too far away.

Mark has curly hair and he wears it cut very short. He loves to ride his skateboard on the footpath in front of our two houses. Sometimes he lets me have a turn.

His brother, Jake, has black hair and dark eyes. He does somersaults on the trampoline in our garden. He is so good at them! He said he'd teach me some tricks on the trampoline. I hope they are easy to do.

*by Molly*

This is another **description**. Remember that descriptions help us to form pictures in our mind of people, places and things. This description uses **personal pronouns** to stand for things that have already been mentioned.

**Personal pronouns** stand for things that have already been mentioned and can be singular (e.g. **I**) or plural (e.g. **they**).

## Let's find them!

**Tip!**

Singular personal pronouns are: **I, me, you, he, him, she, her, it.**
Plural personal pronouns are: **we, us, you, they, them.**

Find the **singular personal pronouns** in the text that stand for the following.

For example: Anna ______ she ______

1. hair ______________________
2. hopscotch ______________________
3. Mark ______________________

Find the **plural personal pronouns** in the text that stand for the following.

4. Molly (understood) and Anna ______________________
5. somersaults ______________________
6. tricks ______________________

# Let's go to the next step!

Are the **personal pronouns** that are underlined in these sentences singular or plural?

For example: They went to the shops to buy some muffins. ___plural___

1. Pass it to me, please. ______________
2. She gave us a salad for lunch and it was very tasty. ______________ ______________
3. I would like a new camera to take a photo of them. ______________ ______________
4. Would you save a cake for my afternoon tea, please Mum? ______________
5. Would you save a cake for my afternoon tea please, Mum and Dad?

   ______________
6. He gave her an umbrella. ______________ ______________

# Let's aim high now!

Complete these sentences with the correct **singular** or **plural pronoun** from the box. The first one has been done for you.

| he | we | them | they | I | she | me |
|---|---|---|---|---|---|---|

1. He sat near ___me___ on the train. [singular]
2. Jake thought he'd lost his bag but ______________ had left it at our house. [singular]
3. I showed my friend, Anna, how to walk to school as ______________ didn't know the way. [singular]
4. The cats who live next door looked hungry so I fed ______________ some milk. [plural]
5. Anna left her skateboard in our garage but ______________ lost it. [plural]
6. I took some flowers to the family next door and ______________ were very pleased. [plural]
7. ______________ like it best when there are children living next door. [singular]

# Let's put it together now!

Find the fifteen **personal pronouns** in this text and put a circle around each of them. The first one has been done for you.

The neighbours from next door have six children. They also have a dog, a cat, chickens, guinea pigs and a turtle. Jenny and I like visiting so we can see all the animals. Mrs Snow lets me feed the dog and cat. She said I could get the eggs from the chickens when I am a bit older. Mrs Snow's eldest son is allowed to get the eggs as he is ten. Jenny likes watching the guinea pigs. She feeds them grass. The turtle moves around very slowly. It isn't afraid of us though. We love having such interesting neighbours as they keep us busy!

# Let's have fun!

Underline the **personal pronouns** in these sentences. Draw a line from the sentence to the picture it describes.

1. John has cooked a cake and it has lots of icing.
2. Would you give me a turn on the skateboard, please?
3. She piled muffins on a plate for the visitors.
4. They ran fast to catch the school bus.
5. Wow! Is that a present for me?

# Let's have a test!

1. Which of the following groups of words are pronouns?

   ◯ house, neighbour, skateboard, tree ◯ went, visited, ate, played
   ◯ her, his, you, I ◯ Molly, Anna, Jake, Bill

In questions 2–3, which pronoun belongs in the sentence?

2. Mr Connor sat down as ______________ was tired from all his cooking.

   ◯ she ◯ he ◯ you ◯ they

3. Which pronoun belongs in this sentence?

   I cooked some popcorn yesterday but I didn't get ______________ hot enough.

   ◯ them ◯ it ◯ us ◯ they

4. Which pronoun stands for the word *Anna* in this sentence?

   I gave the chocolate muffin to Anna as it was the kind ______________ liked.

   ◯ I ◯ her ◯ they ◯ she

5. Which pronoun completes this sentence correctly?

   I sent an invitation to the whole family asking ______________ to my party.

   ◯ they ◯ me ◯ you ◯ them

6. Which pronoun in this sentence is plural?

   I will give him some muffins after I have finished cooking them.

7. Which pronoun in this sentence is singular?

   We took our dog to play with the children next door as she was lonely and we knew they had a dog.

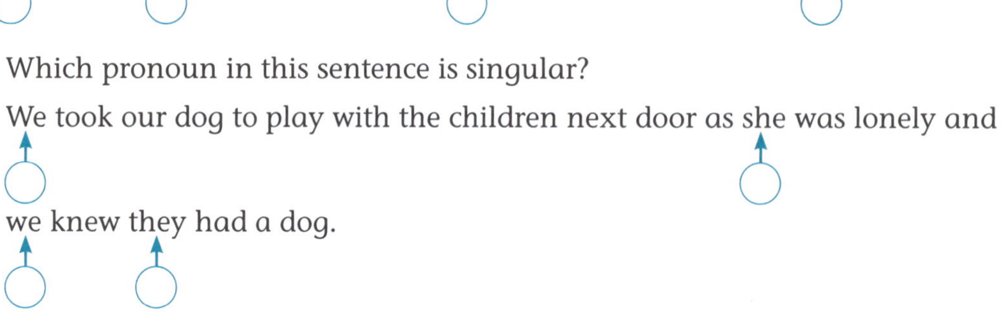

8. Which sentence has a pronoun that could be singular or plural?

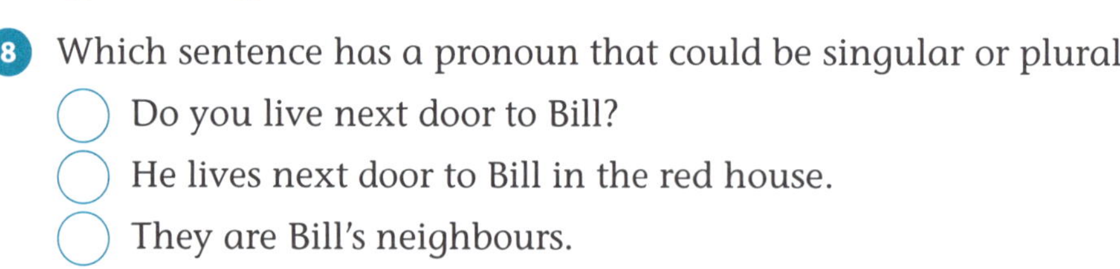

   ◯ Do you live next door to Bill?
   ◯ He lives next door to Bill in the red house.
   ◯ They are Bill's neighbours.
   ◯ I like the neighbours and visit them often.

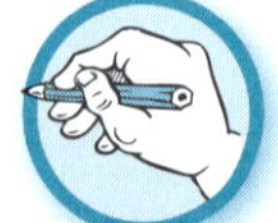

# Let's write now!

Write a **description** of some real or imaginary neighbours. Use **personal pronouns** in your writing to stand for **nouns** that have already been mentioned.

# Unit 7 Hobbies

**Focus**
*Doing and thinking verbs*

## Playing rounders

I **played** rounders yesterday. It is my new hobby.

When Sally **pitched** the ball to me, I swung my bat back hard. Then I swung it forward to hit the ball. I should have hit it, but I missed. I almost fell over!

Jim, the backstop, ran after the ball and threw it back to Sally. She pitched again. The ball went wide. The next pitch looked good to me. I watched it coming then hit it hard. It flew up and away.

"Run, Harry. Run as fast as you can," they called.

I dropped the bat and ran as fast as I could. My ball flew high and fell straight into Sally's hands. I was caught out.

I am going to play much better next time.

*by Harry*

This is another **recount**. **Doing verbs** are used to refer to the actions of Harry and his friends when they are playing rounders.

There are different kinds of verbs. Some verbs are **doing verbs**. They refer to what people or things do; for example, **played**, **pitched**.

## Let's find them!

Find the **doing verb** in the text that refers to the following.

For example: a bowling action ______pitched______

1. an action when moving the bat ____________________
2. connecting the bat to the ball ____________________
3. moving quickly on your feet ____________________
4. letting go of the bat ____________________

5 moving through the air ____________________

6 catching the ball ____________________

## Let's go to the next step!

Choose a **doing verb** from the box to match each group below. The first one has been done for you.

carry hop toss look wait float wobble

1 run, jump, skip, hop

2 throw, pitch, bowl, ____________

3 fall, stumble, trip, ____________

4 fly, soar, glide, ____________

5 watch, stare, see, ____________

6 get, bring, fetch, ____________

7 stop, rest, pause, ____________

## Let's aim high now!

Underline the **doing verbs** in these sentences. The first one has been done for you.

come pitched missed threw fidget wriggle ran wait climbed swung made

1 Sally pitched the ball to me.

2 The children threw their hats in the air when Bill caught the ball.

3 I swung my bat forward but I missed the ball.

4 We ran as fast as we could.

5 I fidget and wriggle when I am bored.

6 Jenny climbed a tree and watched the game.

7 Will you come to the oval for our game tomorrow?

## Choosing a hobby

"Do you **think** I could find a new hobby, Mum?" Tom asked.

"I **guess** so, Tom."

"I really wish I had a hobby."

"What hobbies do your friends have?"

"I forget what Jimbo does. But I remember Bill collects stamps and Amy likes to skateboard."

"Would you like to join a gym club?"

"I wouldn't like that," Tom said.

"I wonder if you'd like to do some gardening?"

"I doubt it," answered Tom.

"What about teaching yourself magic?"

"I think I'd prefer to learn the saxophone."

"I knew you'd think of something. Problem solved," said Tom's mum.

This is another **conversation**. Remember that conversations are spoken exchanges between people. This conversation has been written down. **Thinking verbs** are used to describe Mum's and Tom's different kinds of mental activities.

**Thinking verbs** describe a mental activity rather than a physical activity; for example, **think**, **guess**.

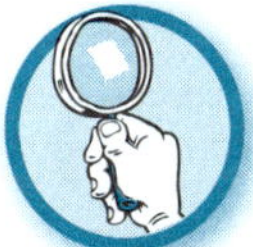

# Let's find them!

You may need to use a dictionary to help you with these questions. Find the **thinking verbs** in the text that begin with the following.

For example: the letter *w* wish

1. the letter *f* ________________
2. the letter *r* ________________
3. the letter *w* ________________
4. the letter *d* ________________
5. the letter *p* ________________
6. the letter *k* ________________

## Let's go to the next step!

Circle the **thinking verb** in each sentence.

For example: I wonder if you could explain how the game is played?

1. I hope you will be in our team.
2. Could you reply quickly if you decide to join our club?
3. I doubt if I can cheer as loudly as that.
4. I suppose I'll have my turn after she has hers.
5. Do you believe she has practised enough to perform at the concert?
6. I can't imagine being brave enough to do that.

## Let's aim high now!

Choose a **thinking verb** from the box to complete each sentence. The first one has been done for you.

| know | decided | realise | hope | imagine | remember | forgot |
|---|---|---|---|---|---|---|

1. I ___hope___ you will teach me how to juggle.
2. Did you ______ Tom is learning the saxophone?
3. She left her skates behind and ______ her gloves as well.
4. I ______ now that I am never going to be a famous ballerina.
5. I can ______ being an astronaut when I grow up.
6. I don't ______ whether you like playing card games.
7. I ______ to learn how to play tiddlywinks.

# Let's put it together now!

Place the **doing** and **thinking verbs** on the part of the body that does each activity on the drawing below.

| think | hop | wonder | watch | bend | jump | see | look |
|---|---|---|---|---|---|---|---|
| draw | kick | turn | stretch | pat | stroke | know | |

# Let's have fun!

Here is a crossword about hobbies. Complete the crossword by choosing the **verb** from the box that goes before the words in the clues.

| knit | ski | collect | play | kicks | make | sing | read | cook | juggle |
|---|---|---|---|---|---|---|---|---|---|

**ACROSS**

3 stamps
5 scarves
7 books
8 songs
9 puppets

**DOWN**

1 on snow
2 a football
3 food
4 cricket
6 balls

| | | | | | | | | | | | | | | | | |
|---|---|---|---|---|---|---|---|---|---|---|---|---|---|---|---|---|
| 1 | | 2 | | | | | 3 | | | | | | | | 4 | |
| 5 | | | | | 6 | | | | | | | | | | | |
| | | | | | | | | | | | | | 7 | | | |
| | | | | | | | | | | | | | | | | |
| | | 8 | | | | | | | | | | | | | | |
| | | | | | | | | | | | | | | | | |
| | | 9 | | | | | | | | | | | | | | |

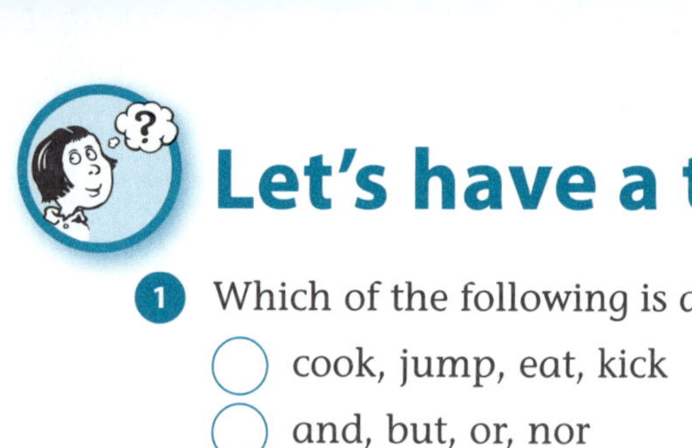

# Let's have a test!

1. Which of the following is a list of doing verbs?
   - ◯ cook, jump, eat, kick
   - ◯ and, but, or, nor
   - ◯ football, baseball, soccer, cricket
   - ◯ weak, tough, soft, hard

2. Which doing verb completes this sentence correctly?

   I like to save stamps and ____________________ them in an album.

   ◯ pour ◯ push ◯ paste ◯ pleat

In questions 3–4, show which of these verbs is a doing verb.

3. ◯ think ◯ throw ◯ ask ◯ imagine

4. ◯ believe ◯ forget ◯ wonder ◯ build

5. Which word in this sentence is a doing verb?

   You skated right across the rink yesterday.

   (◯ skated, ◯ across, ◯ rink, ◯ yesterday)

6. Which word in this sentence is a thinking verb?

   She is a girl guide already as far as I know.

   (◯ girl, ◯ already, ◯ far, ◯ know)

In questions 7–8, which sentence contains a thinking verb?

7. ◯ I hope so. ◯ Did you say that?
   ◯ Will you answer her? ◯ Do you play the violin?

8. ◯ I shall eat my ice-cream after dinner.
   ◯ I threw the boomerang but it didn't come back.
   ◯ Have you decided whether you will come to the game?
   ◯ Will you play cards with me?

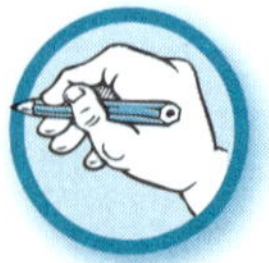

# Let's write now!

Make up a **conversation** between two friends telling each other about their hobbies. Include **doing** and **thinking verbs** in your writing.

# Unit 8 At the farm

**Simple sentences; conjunctions and compound sentences**

## A letter to my grandparents

Dear Gran and Pa,

**We moved to our new farm last week.** I love being here. Please visit us soon. You can see our ducks down at the pond. Sometimes I feed them vegetable scraps.

We mostly have sheep on our farm. Dad said they will have baby lambs in the spring.

My main job is looking after the hens. I collect the eggs from the henhouse. I also lock the hens in the henhouse at night. It keeps them safe from foxes.

Dad gets up at 5 am. Mum and I are still asleep then. Dad sometimes takes the dogs with him out to the paddocks in his jeep. He will buy a tractor soon. He has promised me a ride in it.

See you soon,
Love, Georgie

This is a **letter**. A letter is a written communication addressed to a person or people. Georgie uses **simple sentences** to write to her grandparents about life at her farm.

A **simple sentence** is a group of words that makes sense by itself. It has only one verb. It begins with a capital letter and ends with a full stop; for example, **We moved to our new farm last week.**

## Let's find them!

Find the **simple sentences** in the text which tell the following.

For example:
what you can see at the pond ______ You can see our ducks down at the pond.

1. what Georgie feeds the ducks ______________________________

______________________________

2. which animal they have most of on the farm ______________________________

______________________________

3 why the hens are locked up ______

______

4 when Georgie's dad gets up ______

5 what Georgie's dad will buy ______

______

## Let's go to the next step!

Add a **verb** from the box to the spaces below to make a **simple sentence**. The first one has been done for you.

| sold | chased | moo | fed | went | paddled | chirped |
|---|---|---|---|---|---|---|

1 I ___went___ for a walk to the pond.

2 I ______ the chickens.

3 The baby chicks ______ at their mother.

4 The ducks ______ hard with their feet.

5 We ______ the wool from our sheep.

6 My dog ______ after the fox.

7 Our cows ______ very loudly.

## Let's aim high now!

The words below are in a jumbled order. Re-order them so that they make a **simple sentence**. The first one has been done for you.

1 ride in I had Dad's a tractor. ___I had a ride in Dad's tractor.___

2 duck Sally owns a pet. ______

3 with mother The their swam ducklings. ______

______

4 the cows milks Tom. ______

5 river We the in swim. ______

6 across The dogs paddock raced the. ______

______

7 cabbage in our I grew a garden. ______

______

## Ducks

**Ducks love water and they live near ponds, streams and rivers.** They have webbed feet and they use them as paddles in the water. Ducks eat plants but they also eat fish and worms.

Ducks have waterproof feathers and ducks' feet never get cold. They preen their feathers with their bills. They turn their heads backwards and put their bills into their wings, breast and back.

Most ducks make a quacking noise but not all ducks quack. Some ducks squeal. Female ducks lay eggs and they keep them warm. Ducklings grow feathers quickly and fly at about 2 months old.

This is an **information report**. Remember that information reports give factual information about things. In this report **compound sentences** are used to give information about ducks.

A **conjunction** is a joining word; for example, **and**, **but**. A **compound sentence** is made up of two simple sentences of equal importance, joined by a **conjunction**; for example, **Ducks love water <u>and</u> they live near ponds, streams and rivers.**

# Let's find them!

Find the **compound sentences** in the text that tell about the following. The first one has been done for you.

1. different things ducks eat *Ducks eat plants but they also eat fish and worms.*
2. ducks' feathers and their feet __________
3. the noises made by most ducks __________
4. female ducks' habits __________
5. ducklings' feathers and their flying __________

# Let's go to the next step!

Circle the **conjunctions** in these **compound sentences**.

For example: I rode on the tractor with Dad and I was allowed to steer.

1. Most birds can fly but chickens cannot fly very well.
2. Ducklings waddle behind their mother as they like to keep close to her.
3. Roosters sing cock-a-doodle-doo but chickens can only squawk.
4. Ducks' feathers make good pillows or they can be made into doonas.
5. Goats provide milk and cows provide milk as well.
6. I used to live in the city but now I live on a farm.

# Let's aim high now!

These sentences don't make sense! Draw a line to connect the parts together to make a **compound sentence** that *does* make sense. The first one has been done for you.

| First part of sentence | | Second part of sentence |
|---|---|---|
| Dairy cows eat grass | | and we planted some fruit trees. |
| Pigs have long snouts | | but this little piggy stayed home. |
| This little piggy went to market | | and sold it at the market. |
| It has been very dry | | and they provide most of the world's milk. |
| We dug big holes in the soil | | so we need plenty of rain. |
| They picked the fruit | | and the dam soon filled. |
| The rain fell for seven days | | and they have curly tails. |

# Let's put it together now!

There are ten **conjunctions** in the text. Circle them and then write them on the lines below. The first one has been done for you.

My grandparents came to visit our farm (and) I felt very excited. They had a long journey so they were tired. The next day we walked around the farm together and I showed them the animals. Pa wore his gumboots and he wore a woolly scarf around his neck. Gran had warm gloves and she wore a thick coat. We couldn't find our cat, Milly, but we saw our rooster and the chickens. Gran liked the baby lambs best but Pa liked the ducklings. That evening, Mum lit a fire and Dad lit the lamp. Gran made muffins and I made hot chocolate. The room felt cosy and we were all as warm as toast.

________ ________ ________ ________

________ ________ ________ ________

________ ________

# Let's have fun!

Use the pictures to help you write a **simple sentence** about each kind of farmyard animal. For example, **Ducks love water.**

# Let's have a test!

In questions 1–3, show which word is a conjunction.

1. ◯ jeep ◯ tractor ◯ and ◯ car
2. ◯ chicken ◯ goat ◯ horse ◯ but
3. ◯ or ◯ grass ◯ sore ◯ claw

In questions 4–5, which sentence is a simple sentence?

4. ◯ Tom collected the wool and then he washed it.
   ◯ The cows mooed loudly.
   ◯ The rooster crowed but the hens cackled.
   ◯ I drank some milk but gave the rest to mum.
5. ◯ The goat chewed my cardboard box.
   ◯ The fox got into the henhouse and it scared the chickens.
   ◯ You can see the baby ducklings or you can look at the puppies.
   ◯ The sheep were scared and they huddled together.

In questions 6–7, which sentence is a compound sentence?

6. ◯ Georgie lives on a farm.
   ◯ Georgie looks after the hens and she collects the eggs.
   ◯ Georgie's dad has a tractor on the farm.
   ◯ Georgie loves milk.
7. ◯ The fox sniffed at the gate and pushed his nose under it.
   ◯ She saw the ducks dive under the water.
   ◯ The pigs snuffled in their pens.
   ◯ The duck ate some snails for breakfast.
8. Choose the correct conjunction to complete the sentence.
   I like apples ______________ my brother prefers bananas.
   ◯ because ◯ so ◯ or ◯ but

# Let's write now!

Write an **information report** about a farm animal of your choice. You may need to do some research to find the information you need. Use **simple** and **compound sentences** in reporting your information.

# Unit 9 Recycling

**Focus**
*Verb tense; helping verbs*

## Recycling

Dan: I **want** to recycle my rubbish, Mum.

Mum: Great, Dan. Recycling makes new things out of old rubbish.

Dan: Our teacher says it saves waste and helps the environment.

Mum: You saw those recycle bins outside the shops yesterday, didn't you?

Dan. Yes, I saw them. I put my can in one of them. I **wanted** to add a bottle that I noticed on the pavement but the bin was too full.

Mum: We have four bins at home for general rubbish, garden rubbish, cans and bottles, and paper. The truck picks up the bins and takes them to the recycling depot.

Dan: I think I know what goes in each bin now. Thanks, Mum. I thought you would help me.

This is a **conversation**. Remember that conversations are spoken exchanges between people. Dan and his mother use the **tense of the verbs** to show whether the action happens in the present or the past.

The **tense of a verb** tells us about when an action takes place; for example, **want** (present tense) and **wanted** (past tense). As you can see in this example, verbs can change their form to express their tense.

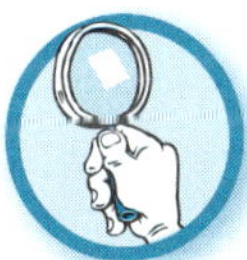

## Let's find them!

Name the **tense** of the underlined **verbs** in the text.

For example: makes ___present___

**Tip!**
Many **verbs** add **ed** to change from **present** to **past tense**; for example, **want** (present), **wanted** (past). But some verbs change their form in other ways; for example, **think** (present), **thought** (past).

1. says ______
2. helps ______
3. saw ______
4. noticed ______
5. have ______
6. think ______
7. thought ______

## Let's go to the next step!

Change the underlined **verbs** in these sentences into the **past tense**.
For example: The teacher hopes to recycle our aluminium cans. hoped

1. She wants us to collect waste paper. ____________________
2. I see the rubbish truck further down the street. ____________________
3. Recycling glass bottles helps us save electricity. ____________________
4. That shopper uses plastic bags to carry her shopping. ____________________
5. I save trees by recycling! ____________________
6. My compost bin fills up quickly. ____________________

## Let's aim high now!

Find the **verb** in these sentences and name its **tense**. Write your answers in the columns below. The first one has been done for you.

**Tip!** Think about whether the action is happening in the present or has happened in the past.

1. These worms want some food scraps.
2. Those wiggly worms ate our vegetable peelings.
3. I used the fertilizer from our compost bin on my cabbages.
4. My uncle has a cane shopping basket with him today.
5. These bottles and jars contain some recycled glass.
6. The material in our compost bin feels damp but not wet.
7. We learned about the environment last term.

| Verb | Tense |
|---|---|
| 1 want | present |
| 2 | |
| 3 | |
| 4 | |
| 5 | |
| 6 | |
| 7 | |

## Recycle and reuse

For years, Bertie Blowitt **has thrown** his rubbish in any old place.

He has left food scraps and cans everywhere. He did not realise how much trouble he was causing.

But Bertie has decided to turn over a new leaf. Now Bertie **is learning** to recycle his rubbish. Every day he is finding different ways to improve the environment.

What about you? Have you thrown used paper into the general rubbish? If so, you were wasting the earth's resources. Did you know that trees are felled to make paper? If you recycle used paper, you are helping to save some trees.

Remember. Do not be like the old Bertie Blowitt. Turn over a new leaf. Recycle and Reuse.

This is a transcript of a radio **advertisement**. Remember that advertisements persuade people to do things. In this advertisement, **helping verbs** are used to tell the story of Bertie's bad habits and to persuade people to recycle their rubbish.

The tense of a verb tells us about when an action takes place. **Helping verbs** can be added to verbs to form tense; for example, **has thrown** (past tense) and **is learning** (present tense).

- Some helping verbs that make the **present tense**: am, is, are, do, does, has, have.
- Some helping verbs that make the **past tense**: was, were, did, has, have, had.

## Let's find them!

**Tip!** When a **helping verb** is added to a **verb** it is called a **verb group**.

Find the **helping verb** and name the **tense** it helps to make in each of the underlined verb groups. The first one has been done for you.

1. has left has, past
2. was causing ____________
3. has decided ____________
4. is finding ____________
5. were wasting ____________
6. are felled ____________
7. are helping ____________

# Let's go to the next step!

Choose a **helping verb** from the box to complete these sentences. The first one has been done for you.

| am | is | are | was | were | had | did |
|---|---|---|---|---|---|---|

1. We ___are___ giving some of our pre-loved clothes to the charity shop.
2. Our school __________ having a swap party today.
3. His family __________ collected fifteen printer cartridges for recycling.
4. I __________ looking forward to National Tree day this year.
5. The company __________ try to reduce its carbon footprint.
6. Dad and mum __________ planning to recycle their old mobile phones but they kept them instead.
7. The first Earth Day __________ held in 1970 in America.

# Let's aim high now!

Write the **verb group** (**helping verb** + **verb**) in column one and its **tense** in column two. The first one has been done for you.

1. We are taking our old tyres to the recycling centre.
2. Her class had collected cans for a whole year.
3. Plastic bags are harming marine life.
4. Bertie is trying to save our planet.
5. We were adding compost to the soil yesterday.
6. Susan's family is going to buy a worm farm.
7. She was putting her rubbish in the wrong bin.

| Verb group | Tense |
|---|---|
| 1 are taking | present |
| 2 | |
| 3 | |
| 4 | |
| 5 | |
| 6 | |
| 7 | |

# Let's put it together now!

Read the text below and then change the bolded **verbs** or **verb groups** from the **present** to the **past tense**. Write your answers in the columns below. The first one has been done for you.

**What am I?**

Mel **does** his homework on me. The next day Mel **takes** me to school. His teacher **tells** him to show me to her. She **looks** at me and then **says** to Mel, "Very good." Mel **puts** me in his desk.

At the end of the year, Mel **clears** out his desk. He **decides** to throw me away. His teacher **tells** him to put me in the recycle bin. Hurrah! I **am going** to be made new again.

**Answer:** I am a piece of paper.

| Present tense | Past tense |
|---|---|
| does | did |
| takes | |
| tells | |
| looks | |
| says | |
| puts | |
| clears | |
| decides | |
| tells | |
| am going | |

# Let's have fun!

The verb group is missing from these Earth Hour messages. Find the missing **verb group** from the box and put it into the correct place in each thought balloon.

am going Have seen was begun have used

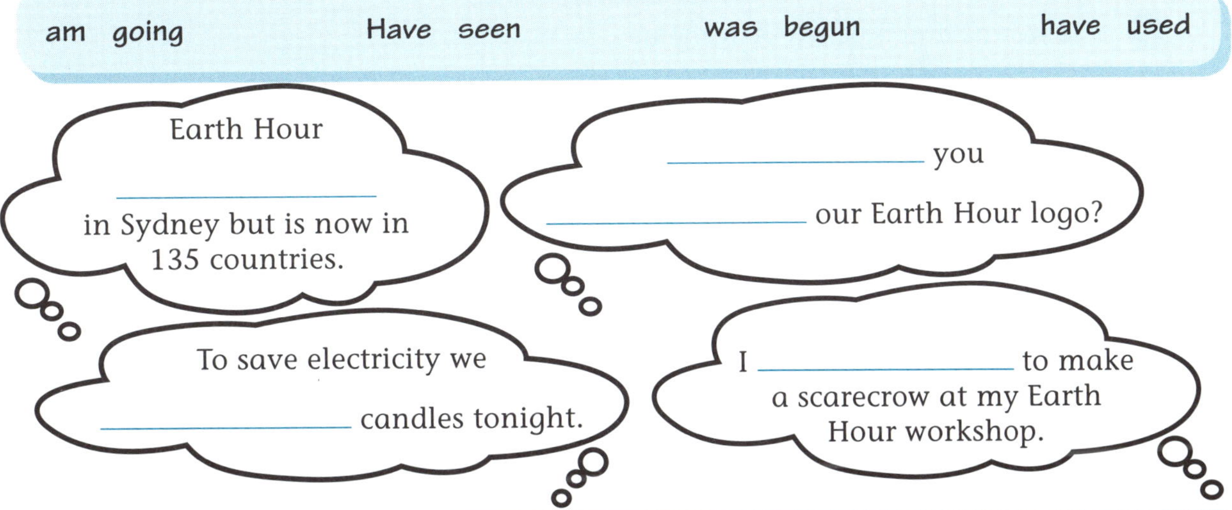

# Let's have a test!

1. What is the present tense of saved?

◯ saw ◯ saving ◯ saver ◯ save

In questions 2–3, which word is in the past tense?

2. ◯ worked ◯ working ◯ worker ◯ workers

3. ◯ thinked ◯ thunk ◯ thought ◯ thinks

4. Which is the present tense verb in this sentence?

I gave her a hessian bag but I think she lost it last week.

5. Which is the past tense verb in this sentence?

He wanted those vegetable scraps for the compost bin.

In questions 6–8, which is the helper verb in the sentence?

6. There is a compost bin at our farm that was made by my brother.

7. To have our own fertilizer, we are making a worm farm.

8. The worms had finished their meal.

# Let's write now!

Create an **advertisement** to encourage people to do something special to help save our planet. Take care to use **tenses** correctly.

# Unit 10 Aboriginal culture

**Focus**
*Saying, being and having verbs*

## Lost in Kakadu

"I think we are lost," I **murmured** to Sammy.

"Help!" Sammy yelped. "Kakadu covers nearly 20,000 square kilometres!"

"Where is our map?" I asked.

"I think I left it back at the camp," Sammy sighed.

"We might have to stay overnight," I whispered.

"What will we eat though? We don't know how to hunt like the Aboriginal people," he said.

Just then we passed a rock I recognised.

"Wasn't this the rock we thought could be the Aboriginal creation ancestor?" I suggested.

"Yes. Hurrah!" Sammy shouted. "We are saved. We can track our footsteps back from here."

This is a **narrative**. A narrative tells a story. **Saying** verbs are used to express different ways Sammy and his friend say things in their story.

**Saying verbs** express different ways of saying; for example, **murmured**.

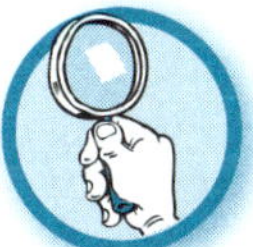

## Let's find them!

Find six more **saying verbs** used by Sammy and his friend in the story.
For example: yelped

1. ______
2. ______
3. ______
4. ______
5. ______
6. ______

# Let's go to the next step!

Circle the **saying verbs** in these sentences.

For example: "I love the sound of Aboriginal words," she (said).

1. "Do you know the Aboriginal name for a monsoon?" I asked.
2. Our teacher told us Aboriginal people have lived in Kakadu for thousands of years.
3. I whispered that the East Alligator river sounds scary!
4. Some people argue that sunset is a good time to see wildlife.
5. Susan promised we could see the dragon lizards.
6. The ranger explained there is a storm season in Kakadu.

# Let's aim high now!

Choose a **saying verb** from the box to complete these sentences. The first one has been done for you.

| pleaded | asked | said | announced | told | groaned | described |
|---|---|---|---|---|---|---|

1. I ____told____ my little sister about the traditional owners of Kakadu.
2. The ranger __________ that the monsoon season is an interesting time.
3. I __________ when I heard there are millions of insects in Kakadu!
4. The tourist __________ how to get to Kakadu.
5. I __________ the beautiful water lilies I'd seen in Kakadu National Park.
6. "Please, please, can't we stay camping here longer," I __________.
7. He __________ that a new Aboriginal rock painting had been found.

## Aboriginal art

Many Aboriginal paintings tell stories of the Dreamtime. These stories **are** about creation. They are about how the land came into being.

The traditional paint colouring Aboriginal people use is from pigments found in the soil, and from clay and charcoal. Rocks, bark and the walls of caves were places where they often painted their stories.

Patterns are important in their paintings. For example, Aboriginal paintings often **have** patterns of white dots. These dots, and their placement, have particular meanings. There are symbols that stand for man, woman, track, kangaroo, waterhole and so on.

Today, galleries all over the world display Aboriginal paintings in their collections.

*by Abby*

This is another **information report**. In this report, Abby uses **being** and **having verbs** to tell about Aboriginal art.

**Being verbs** are about what things are while **having verbs** are about what things have. They stand on their own without being part of a verb group; for example, stories **are** about creation; paintings often **have** patterns.

# Let's find them!

Find seven **being** and **having verbs** (other than the examples) in the text about Aboriginal art. The first one has been done for you.

1. are
2. ______
3. ______
4. ______
5. ______
6. ______
7. ______

**Tip!**

Being verbs: **am, is, are, was, were**
Having verbs: **have, has, had**

# Let's go to the next step!

Circle the **being verbs** in these sentences.

For example: Brown, yellow and orange (are) earth colours.

1. One of the Aboriginal symbols for a possum is like a capital E.
2. That circle, with another circle inside it, is the symbol for a campsite.
3. The wombat was beside the emu in that painting.
4. Some of those cave paintings were over 20,000 years old.
5. This is an Aboriginal painting.
6. I am sure those marks stand for footprints.

# Let's aim high now!

Choose a **being** or a **having verb** from the box to complete these sentences. The first one has been done for you.

| is | has | Were | have | was | are | is |
|---|---|---|---|---|---|---|

1. A painting called 'Kangaroo' _____is_____ by a famous Aboriginal artist.
2. Aboriginal people __________ a long history of creating art.
3. There __________ an Aboriginal dot painting at the exhibition yesterday.
4. This bark from a gum tree __________ an Aboriginal painting on it.
5. That __________ a picture of the creation of a river.
6. __________ you there when he was painting the outside of the didgeridoo?
7. The colours in his painting __________ all earth colours.

# Let's put it together now!

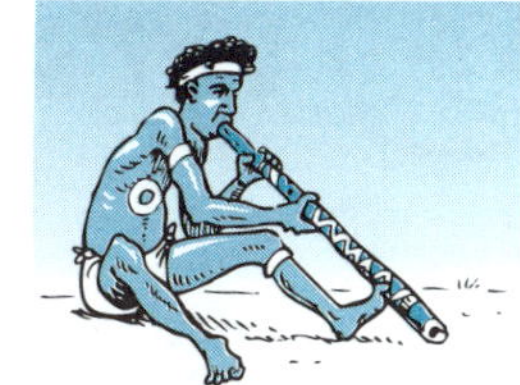

Find five **saying verbs**, four **being verbs** and three **having verbs** in this story about watching an Aboriginal corroboree. Write them in the columns below. The first set has been done for you.

I watched a corroboree held by Aboriginal people. I asked Mum why the children danced with their elders. She explained that Aboriginal children, from a very early age, have a role in many of these ceremonies. Most of the performers had body paint on their bodies.

There were colourful costumes and chanting. I heard a wonderful deep sound with a strong beat. It was from a didgeridoo. Dad said it is one of the oldest instruments in the world.

He also told me that an Aboriginal word for a corroboree is 'kobbakobba'. I repeated that word over and over when I heard it. I had a wonderful time at the corroboree.

| Saying verbs | Being verbs | Having verbs |
|---|---|---|
| 1 asked | 1 were | 1 have |
| 2 | 2 | 2 |
| 3 | 3 | 3 |
| 4 | 4 | |
| 5 | | |

# Let's have fun!

The clues will help you work out the **saying**, **being** and **having verbs** that complete this crossword. For some of the answers you can choose a word from the brackets.

**Across**

2. I ______________ sick yesterday. (was/were)
3. This word means 'call out loudly'.
4. He ______________ toothache now. (has, had)
7. This word means 'said you definitely will'.
8. I ______________ a dream last night. (has/had)

**Down**

1. This verb means 'requests'.
2. This verb means 'spoke softly'.
5. They ______________ not here. (are, was)
6. I ____________ better now. (am, is)

| 1 | | | | | | 2 | | |
|---|---|---|---|---|---|---|---|---|
| 3 | | | | | | | | |
| | | | | | | | | |
| | | | | 4 | | | | |
| | 5 | | 6 | | | | | |
| 7 | | | | | | | | |
| | | | | | | | | |
| | | | | | | | | |
| | | | | 8 | | | | |

# Let's have a test!

1. Which is the saying verb in this sentence?

   I told you not to stand in front of me.

   ◯ told ◯ not ◯ stand ◯ front

2. Which sentence has a saying verb?

   ◯ You can see the river below us.
   ◯ She asked where the river began.
   ◯ This river is the home of the Rainbow Serpent.
   ◯ We are having a picnic by the river.

3. Which saying verb completes this sentence correctly?

   It was ______________ in 1981 that Kakadu was now a World Heritage site.

   ◯ announced ◯ muttered ◯ whispered ◯ asked

4. Which is the being verb in this sentence?

   The corroboree is a very colourful ceremony.

   ◯ corroboree ◯ is ◯ very ◯ ceremony

5. Which sentence contains a being verb?

   ◯ He plays the didgeridoo.
   ◯ The didgeridoo sounds wonderful.
   ◯ The didgeridoo was very old.
   ◯ I want to learn the didgeridoo.

6. Which being verb is needed to complete this sentence?

   They ______________ at the corroboree now.

   ◯ is ◯ are ◯ was ◯ were

7. Which having verb is needed to complete this sentence?

   He ______________ not played the clapsticks until I showed him how.

   ◯ has ◯ had ◯ have ◯ having

8. Which sentence has a having verb?

   ◯ The Rainbow Serpent is a sacred animal.
   ◯ I read a story about the Rainbow Serpent.
   ◯ The Rainbow Serpent has beautiful colours.
   ◯ Where does the Rainbow Serpent live?

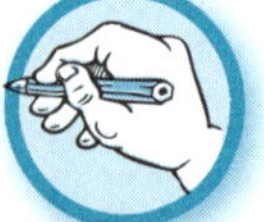

# Let's write now!

Write your own **story** about an adventure in a rainforest. Use **saying verbs** to show the different ways people speak to each other.

# Unit 11 Story time

*Adverbs*

## Stolen treasure

I had to find them **quickly** before anyone else did!

I slid **silently** along the wall towards the window. The robbers were inside arguing noisily. I bent low and crawled slowly past the window on my hands and knees. Agggh! I knocked my head hard against the window sill as I stood up. I stayed still.

Had anyone heard? I didn't think so as the robbers were singing and shouting loudly now. It felt scary!

I crept further towards the shed. This must be where they had hidden the jewels. I pulled hard at the door but it wouldn't open. It seemed to be stuck fast. Out with my pocket knife! I played with the lock and luckily it broke.

I hope I find the jewels soon. I don't want to be caught here.

This is another **narrative**. The author uses **adverbs** with verbs to give more information about the way things happen in this story about stolen treasure.

**Adverbs** are words that can add meaning to verbs and give more information; for example, find **quickly**, slid **silently**.

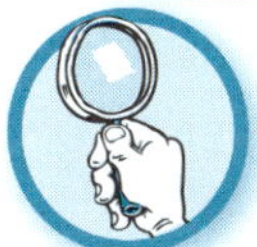

## Let's find them!

**Tip!** Adverbs often end in **ly**.

Find the **adverbs** in the text which add meaning to the following verbs.

For example: arguing noisily

1. crawled ______________________
2. knocked ______________________
3. stayed ______________________
4. shouting ______________________
5. stuck ______________________
6. broke ______________________

# Let's go to the next step!

Choose an **adverb** from the box that adds meaning to the underlined **verbs**. Write it in the space to complete each sentence. The first one has been done for you.

| sadly | quietly | slowly | quickly | angrily | closely | loudly |
|---|---|---|---|---|---|---|

1. Jack <u>shook</u> his fist angrily.
2. The teacher <u>told</u> the children to sit ______________ while she read to them.
3. The tortoise <u>moves</u> more ______________ than the hare.
4. She <u>looked</u> ______________ at the wounded bird.
5. I <u>walked</u> ______________ to the library because I didn't want to be late.
6. I like mum and dad to <u>sit</u> ______________ beside me when I'm watching a scary TV show.
7. Please <u>read</u> more ______________ so we can all hear.

# Let's aim high now!

Underline the **verbs** in these sentences and circle the **adverbs** that add to their meaning.
For example: The witch <u>sneered</u> (cruelly) at Gretel.

1. We sat comfortably while our teacher read *King Kong* to us.
2. Cinderella ran swiftly towards the prince.
3. Mother Bear spoke crossly to Little Bear.
4. Jack stared angrily at the cruel giant.
5. The ugly sisters laughed merrily as they watched Cinderella scrub the floor.
6. Augustus accidentally fell into the chocolate lake.

## Book Week parade

When the bell rang, we moved **quickly** into our lines. It was time for our Book Week parade. Everyone was dressed differently from usual. We were dressed as characters from books. Some characters seemed real!

We **soon** hurried into the library and looked proudly at the displays we had made. Then we sat in groups and listened to stories.

Finally, our parade began. I was dressed as Pippi Longstocking. My friend, Jess, was Captain Hook. She waved her hook and snarled nastily at her friends! My brother, Bill, had come as the Lorax.

The winner of the Book Week parade was Sarah. She had come as the giant from *Jack and the Beanstalk*. She looked tall because she was balancing cleverly on stilts hidden under her costume.

*by Jake*

This is a **recount**. Remember that a recount tells about things that have already happened. Jake uses **adverbs** to tell us about how or when things happened at the Book Week parade.

**Adverbs** can tell how or when something happens; for example, moved **quickly** tells how they moved; **soon** hurried tells when they hurried.

# Let's find them!

**Tip!**

Ask a *how* or *when* question about the **verb** to find the **adverb**; for example, how did they move? They moved **quickly**. When did they hurry? They **soon** hurried.

Find the **adverbs** in the text that tell how or when in the following.

For example:
everyone was dressed differently

1. some characters seemed ____________
2. the children looked at the displays ____________
3. the children sat in groups ____________
4. the parade began ____________
5. Jess snarled ____________
6. Sarah was balancing ____________

# Let's go to the next step!

Find the **adverbs** in the sentences that tell how or when about the underlined **verbs**. Write them in the columns below. The first one has been done for you.

1. The Aboriginal elder kindly <u>told</u> us a Dreaming story.
2. Mum soon <u>remembered</u> her mum had read her *Peter Rabbit*.
3. Do you know that book where the caterpillar <u>eats</u> hungrily through the pages?
4. Afterwards, the teacher <u>read</u> us *Charlie and the Chocolate Factory*.
5. The wolf <u>blew</u> hard at the pig's house hoping to blow it down.
6. Pippi Longstocking had already <u>lifted</u> her horse with only one hand.
7. Suddenly, she <u>shrank</u> to the size of a pepperpot.

| Adverb | Tells how or when? |
|---|---|
| 1 kindly | how |
| 2 | |
| 3 | |
| 4 | |
| 5 | |
| 6 | |
| 7 | |

# Let's aim high now!

Find the **verbs** in these sentences. Then find the **adverbs** that tell how or when about the verbs and write them in the columns below. The first one has been done for you.

1. Afterwards, they joined the parade.
2. We left hurriedly for the book parade.
3. The wicked troll threw a chair violently against the wall.
4. Stand quietly in your costumes for a few minutes, please.
5. Dad often reads us a bedtime story.
6. Let me fix your moustache properly.
7. Leave now!

| Adverb | Tells how or when? |
|---|---|
| 1 afterwards | when |
| 2 | |
| 3 | |
| 4 | |
| 5 | |
| 6 | |
| 7 | |

# Let's put it together now!

Complete this story by putting the **adverbs** from the box into the spaces. The first line has been done for you.

again greedily slyly boldly suspiciously Next crossly shyly

The mother rabbit glared crossly at her babies.

"Who has ______________ eaten my carrots?" she asked.

No answer from her babies.

"Who has stolen my carrots?" she asked ______________.

"Not me," the timid baby rabbit said ______________.

"Not me," the brave baby rabbit answered ______________.

The mother stared ______________ at them. ______________ she asked, "Where are the twins?"

The baby rabbits ______________ stole a look at each other. They knew where the twins were hiding! But they were not going to tell.

# Let's have fun!

Look closely at the expressions and body language of the people in the pictures below. Imitate their expressions and movements to get the feeling of how they are behaving. Now draw a line from each sentence to the picture it matches.

1. He sneered cruelly.
2. I am running late.
3. You yawned rudely.
4. She slept soundly.
5. They danced joyfully.

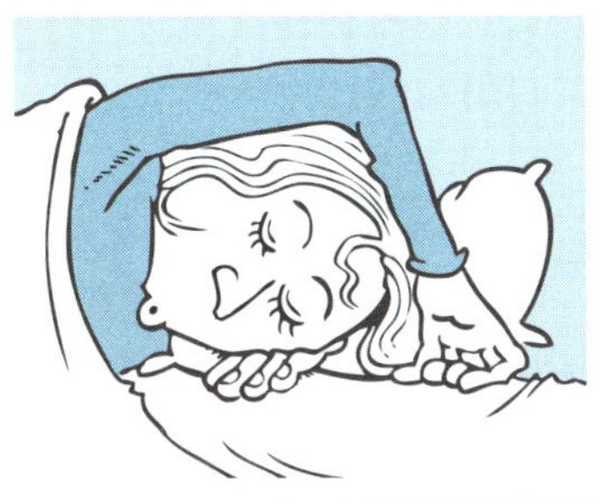

# Let's have a test!

In questions 1–2, choose the sentence which has an adverb.

**1**
- ◯ I read her a story.
- ◯ I read him a story.
- ◯ I read the story aloud.
- ◯ I read the story to the class.

**2**
- ◯ Jack climbed the beanstalk quickly.
- ◯ Jack climbed the beanstalk.
- ◯ Jack shinned up the beanstalk.
- ◯ Jack didn't want to climb the beanstalk.

In questions 3–4, choose the sentence which has an adverb that tells when.

**3**
- ◯ I think she slept soundly.
- ◯ The prince kissed her cheek gently.
- ◯ She woke from her sleep today!
- ◯ The prince was pleased she had woken.

**4**
- ◯ The helicopter landed unsteadily.
- ◯ The plane took off immediately.
- ◯ The train roared noisily out of the station.
- ◯ The brakes on his car sounded creepy.

**5** Complete this sentence with an adverb that tells when.

The children are listening to the story ______________.

- ◯ quietly
- ◯ silently
- ◯ happily
- ◯ now

In questions 6–8, choose the sentence which has an adverb that tells how.

**6**
- ◯ The princess slept late.
- ◯ The pea was secretly hidden under the princess's mattresses.
- ◯ The princess couldn't feel the pea.
- ◯ Have you ever read *The Princess and the Pea*?

**7**
- ◯ The Rainbow Serpent slid smoothly across the hillside.
- ◯ The Rainbow Serpent tried to find his tribe.
- ◯ The Rainbow Serpent soon crossed the land.
- ◯ I always love stories about the Rainbow Serpent.

**8**
- ◯ Charlotte the spider rescued Wilbur the pig.
- ◯ Charlotte the spider wanted to rescue Wilbur the pig.
- ◯ Charlotte the spider soon rescued Wilbur the pig.
- ◯ Charlotte the spider cleverly rescued Wilbur the pig.

# Let's write now!

Write the **story** of a well-known fairytale from the point of view of the 'baddie'. Include **adverbs** that make your story sound lively and vivid.

# Unit 12 Pets

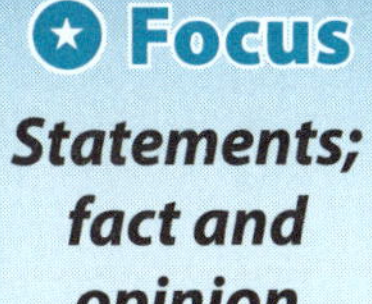


***Statements; fact and opinion***

## Pets

**A pet is an animal kept in people's homes**. People like to have pets for company. Pets are often loyal and loving.

Dogs and cats are very popular pets. Other animals that people keep in their homes include mice, rabbits, guinea pigs, birds and fish. Turtles, lizards and even snakes are sometimes kept as pets. Which pet would you choose?

Children like to have their own pets. Each pet has different needs. Dogs need to be taken for a walk every day. Mice and rabbits need to have their cages kept clean. Kittens like to play with toys.

Pets need care. They give their owners trust in return.

This is another **information report**. Remember that information reports give factual information about things. In this report **statements** are used to give information about pets.

**Statements** are sentences that give information; for example, **A pet is an animal kept in people's homes**.

## Let's find them!

**Tip!** **Statements** always start with a **capital letter** and end with a **full stop**.

Find the **statements** in the text that give information about the following.

For example:
why people like to have pets ___People like to have pets for company.___

1. which pets are very popular ______________________

______________________

2. what children like ______________________

______________________

3. what each pet has ______________________________

______________________________

4. what kittens like ______________________________

5. what pets need ______________________________

## Let's go to the next step!

Choose a word from the box to make these into **statements**. The first one has been done for you.

| babies | lead | fed | dog | whistle | nibble | me |
|---|---|---|---|---|---|---|

1. My canary likes to ___whistle___.
2. I put on Bruno's ______________ for his walk.
3. I ______________ your rabbit for you yesterday.
4. My goldfish likes to ______________ at its food.
5. Her cat scratched ______________.
6. Our guinea pigs have had ______________.
7. My cat hisses at the ______________ from next door.

## Let's aim high now!

Which of these are **statements**? Write 'statement' or 'not a statement' beside each sentence on the lines below.

For example: I saw her new puppy. ___statement___

1. Did you see her new puppy? ______________
2. Will you please give her dog a bone? ______________
3. She gave her dog a bone. ______________
4. Has the kitten had its dinner? ______________
5. The guinea pigs ate all the grass beneath their cage. ______________
6. Do you take your dog for walks? ______________

## My new kitten

You will never guess. **I was given a kitten for my birthday.** When I woke up I went downstairs. My new kitten was asleep in her basket in the laundry. **I thought she looked beautiful.**

My kitten is twelve weeks old. Dad told me she had to stay with her mother for the first weeks of her life. Kittens need their mother's milk to grow strong. I think she will miss her brothers and sisters for a while.

When my kitten woke up she ran about all over the house. She tried to catch her tail. Then she played with a ball of string that she found behind the couch. She made my family laugh.

I filled her bowl with milk. Then I showed her the kitty litter. I think she will learn to use it quickly.

*by Asha*

This is another **recount**. Asha uses statements of **fact** and **opinion** in telling about getting a new kitten.

**Statements** can give **facts** (e.g. **I was given a kitten for my birthday**) or they can offer an **opinion** (e.g. **I thought she looked beautiful**).

## Let's find them!

**Tip!**

Words such as **I think**, **I thought**, **I believe**, **In my view** and **I hope** are used to introduce an **opinion**.

Find the **statements** in the text that give information about the following.

For example: the kitten's age My kitten is twelve weeks old.

1. what kittens need ______________________________

______________________________

2. what the kitten tried to catch ______________________________

______________________________

3. how the family reacted when they watched the kitten ______________________________

______________________________

4 what was put in the kitten's bowl ______________________________

______________________________

5 when the kitten will learn to use kitty litter ______________________________

______________________________

## Let's go to the next step!

Write **fact** or **opinion** beside the following statements.
For example: Kittens grow into cats. ______fact______

1 Kittens have two eyes. ______________________________

2 I think my kitten is the prettiest cat in our street. ______________________________

3 In my view, mother cats like it when their kittens grow up. ______________________________

4 Kittens have soft hair and a tail. ______________________________

5 Kittens are more fun than puppies. ______________________________

6 Many baby animals need to be cared for. ______________________________

## Let's aim high now!

Choose the words from the box to complete the **statements**. Then write whether the statements are **fact** or **opinion** on the lines. The first one has been done for you.

| beautiful | kittens | tail | think | view | anything | need |
|---|---|---|---|---|---|---|

1 Very young ___kittens___ need their mother's milk to stay healthy. ______fact______

2 In my ______________ people shouldn't have any pets. ______________

3 I ______________ pets are too much trouble. ______________

4 Mice ______________ to have their cages cleaned out. ______________

5 Kittens are ______________. ______________

6 Kittens have a ______________. ______________

7 Having a pet is better than ______________. ______________

# Let's put it together now!

The statements below are a mix of **fact** and **opinion**. Put a blue line through the statements that are facts and a green line through the statements that are opinions. There should be six of each.

Guinea pigs have hairy coats.

I think my guinea pig might bite me.

Guinea pigs don't have tails.

Guinea pigs are kind.

Rabbits are always friendly.

Rabbits live in burrows.

Rabbits have long ears.

Rabbits make most people sneeze.

Goldfish have gills.

In my view goldfish should all be set free.

Goldfish live in freshwater.

Goldfish are very smart animals.

# Let's have fun!

Draw a pet you have or would like to have. Write down five **statements** about your pet and link them to the drawing. Your statements can be **fact** (e.g. My dog has four legs) or **opinion** (e.g. My dog has beautiful eyes).

# Let's have a test!

In questions 1–2, choose the sentence which is a statement.

**1**
- ◯ What is in her basket?
- ◯ Will you pass me my dog's lead, please?
- ◯ The goldfish is in her bowl.
- ◯ Did you let her on the couch?

**2**
- ◯ Would you give that to me, please?
- ◯ Are you able to throw him the ball?
- ◯ Didn't I ask you to stay away from there?
- ◯ I hope you won't wake my kitten.

In questions 3–5, which statement gives factual information?

**3**
- ◯ I think dogs are easier to look after than cats.
- ◯ I think cats are easier to look after than dogs.
- ◯ Very young kittens drink milk from their mother.
- ◯ In my view puppies should not drink too much milk.

**4**
- ◯ Horses have four legs.
- ◯ Goldfish look very clever.
- ◯ Kittens have pretty faces.
- ◯ Puppies like trampolining.

**5**
- ◯ Guinea pigs are such fun.
- ◯ Monkeys make very sweet pets.
- ◯ Billy goats look very cross.
- ◯ Some birds are kept in cages.

In questions 6–8, which statement is an opinion?

**6**
- ◯ Dogs and cats are popular pets in many countries.
- ◯ Rabbits make the best pets in the world.
- ◯ Guinea pigs have hairy coats.
- ◯ Canaries often have yellow feathers.

**7**
- ◯ Horses are ridden by people
- ◯ It is unkind to keep birds in cages.
- ◯ Guinea pigs eat grass.
- ◯ Dogs and cats have tails.

**8**
- ◯ People look after their pets very well in my view.
- ◯ Dogs need plenty of exercise.
- ◯ Hens lay eggs.
- ◯ Guide Dogs are trained to help blind people.

# Let's write now!

Write an **information report** about an animal that can be kept as a pet such as a dog, goldfish, canary or guinea pig. You may need to look up your choice of animal to find out more about it. Include **statements of fact** in your report.

# Unit 13 Museums

**Focus**

*Prepositions; prepositional phrases*

## Museums

Most museums are **in** large cities. They are used to store things from the past. People visit museums to see what is on display.

Objects are often placed around the walls of the rooms. There might be old toys such as pedal cars or lead soldiers. You might see very early machines on the shelves such as a computer or a radio. Sometimes precious objects are kept inside glass cases.

When people come into a museum they can take a map from the information desk. This will show them what is kept in the different rooms. Museums can also be visited on the Internet.

This is another **information report**. Remember that information reports give factual information about things. This report uses **prepositions** to tell us about the position of things in museums.

**Prepositions** tell us about the position of people, animals, places and things; for example, museums are **in** large cities.

## Let's find them!

Find ten **prepositions** in the text and write them on the lines below. The first one has been done for you.

**Tip!**

Common **prepositions** include **above**, **across**, **after**, **along**, **around**, **at**, **behind**, **below**, **beneath**, **beside**, **between**, **by**, **during**, **from**, **in**, **inside**, **into**, **near**, **next to**, **of**, **off**, **on**, **onto**, **outside**, **over**, **through**, **to**, **under**, **underneath**, **until** and **with**.

1. from
2. ______
3. ______
4. ______
5. ______
6. ______
7. ______
8. ______
9. ______
10. ______

# Let's go to the next step!

Choose a **preposition** from the box to complete these sentences. The first one has been done for you.

| until | beside | on | in | at | to | from |
|---|---|---|---|---|---|---|

1. We are going to the museum ____on____ Monday.
2. The museum closes ________ 8 pm.
3. Bark paintings are placed ________ boomerangs in the Aboriginal section.
4. The spitfire is hung ________ the ceiling.
5. The new museum was opened ________ 2010.
6. You have to travel ________ Canberra to see that museum.
7. The cafe does not open ________ next week.

# Let's aim high now!

Circle the **prepositions** in the sentences below.

For example: I saw an Egyptian mummy (in) the British Museum.

1. The paintings were hung above the wooden cabinet.
2. Our local museum is across the river.
3. You can see a very old bark canoe near that wall.
4. My great-grandfather's medals are spread along the shelf.
5. We visited a historic house that was built by the water.
6. That brooch, beside the necklace, is a thousand years old.

## A letter to Yoko

25th May

Hi Yoko

Yesterday, **in the afternoon**, I went **to the toy museum**. It is near the railway station. I hope you can visit it next month.

It has interesting toys from the past. You could not get bored even if you tried! In the entrance there are three model spitfire fighter planes. The biggest one is hung from the ceiling.

There are many old toys in the other rooms. My favourites were the lead soldiers and the pedal car. There was a notice hanging on the wall saying "Please do not touch the toys." But there were some toys you could play with in the corner.

I'll be home in a few days and will tell you more then.

Love, Harry

This is another **letter**. Harry uses **prepositional phrases** in his letter to tell when and where.

**Prepositional phrases** are groups of words. They begin with a preposition and do not have a verb. They can tell when and where. For example, **in the afternoon** tells when the person went to the museum; **to the toy museum** tells where the person went.

## Let's find them!

Find the **prepositional phrases** in the text that tell the following.

For example: where the museum is near the railway station

1. when Harry hopes Yoko can visit the museum __________
2. when the toys are from __________
3. where the spitfires are __________
4. where the old toys are __________

5. where the notice was hanging ______________________

6. when Harry will be home ______________________

## Let's go to the next step!

Complete the **phrase** in each sentence with **prepositions** from the box that tell you where. The first one has been done for you.

| next to | with | on | inside | at | in | underneath |
|---|---|---|---|---|---|---|

1. After our visit, we had lunch ___underneath___ the shade of a tree.
2. A display of lead soldiers was placed ______________ the war medals.
3. You can see tiny Japanese sculptures ______________ that shelf.
4. A collection of teddy bears was kept ______________ the other soft toys.
5. There are very few toy museums ______________ Australia.
6. There were six little dinky cars locked ______________ a glass cabinet.
7. I left my umbrella ______________ the museum.

## Let's aim high now!

Do the **prepositional phrases** in these sentences tell where or when?

For example: He saw an old meccano set <u>at the museum</u>. ___where___

1. She and Yoko are going <u>next week</u>. ______________
2. My grandpa has some dinky toys <u>in his study</u>. ______________
3. I have a collection of soft toys <u>in my room</u>. ______________
4. That museum has school visits <u>in the afternoon</u>. ______________
5. Some of the displays were hung <u>on the walls</u>. ______________
6. Are you coming with Yoko <u>on Tuesday</u>? ______________

# Let's put it together now!

Add these drawings to the picture below.

- a book **on** the table
- a vase of flowers **beside** the book
- a pair of glasses **on top of** the book
- a chair **next to** the table
- a shoe **under** the chair
- a mouse **near** the shoe
- two butterflies **above** the table

# Let's have fun!

Harry sent Yoko some **instructions** about how to get from her motel to the room of old toys in the museum. How many **prepositional phrases** does he use? Write the answer in the space in the sentence below.

**Instructions:** Come out of the motel and turn to the right. Walk along the path, over the hill and across the road. Go up the steps, into the museum and past the counter. Go through the doorway and turn to the right. Go in the second door and you will be in the room that has the old toys.

**Answer:** There are ____________________ prepositional phrases in Harry's instructions.

## Let's have a test!

1. Which sentence has a preposition?

- ◯ She bought an entry ticket.
- ◯ Her ticket was expensive.
- ◯ Her entry ticket cost a dollar.
- ◯ She paid for her ticket at the window.

In questions 2–4, choose the word that completes the sentence correctly.

2. She looked at the painting which was hung ________________ the window.

- ◯ between
- ◯ in
- ◯ beside
- ◯ on

3. I want to visit that new museum ________________ the river.

- ◯ in
- ◯ across
- ◯ under
- ◯ inside

4. She hung the straps of her bag ________________ the hook.

- ◯ underneath
- ◯ over
- ◯ beside
- ◯ during

5. Which sentence tells where the Space Museum is?

- ◯ The Space Museum is very popular.
- ◯ The Space Museum is in Washington.
- ◯ The Space Museum is closed.
- ◯ The Space Museum is open today.

6. Which sentence tells where you can find websites for museums?

- ◯ Museums often have websites.
- ◯ Museums have websites on the Internet.
- ◯ I like to visit museum websites.
- ◯ I looked at a museum website last week.

7. Which sentence tells when you can take a guided tour of the National Museum?

- ◯ The National Museum has hundreds of visitors daily.
- ◯ The National Museum is in Canberra.
- ◯ The National Museum is closed for guided tours.
- ◯ The National Museum has guided tours on Sundays.

8. Which sentence tells when the Golden Dragon museum is open?

- ◯ The Golden Dragon Museum is in Bendigo, Victoria.
- ◯ We visited the Golden Dragon Museum last year.
- ◯ The Golden Dragon Museum opens every day.
- ◯ They serve yum cha at the Golden Dragon Museum cafe.

## Let's write now!

Write an **information report** about a museum you have visited or have looked at on the Internet. Use **prepositional phrases** that tell when and where things are placed in your museum.

# Unit 14 On the stage

**Focus**
***Speech marks; commas***

## Magic tricks

**"Come here, Greenie,"** says Pinkie.

"What do you want, Pinkie?" asks Greenie.

"I think you stole my black cat," says Pinkie.

"Shhh. Someone will hear you!" whispers Greenie.

"I hope they do. You are a thief, Greenie. Why don't you own up?"

"I am not a thief. But I think I know what happened to your cat."

"What do you think happened, then?" asks Pinkie.

"The blue witch cast a spell on your cat. She made it invisible!"

"I don't believe you," Pinkie replies.

"Listen carefully. What do you hear?" asks Greenie.

"Miaow, miaow, miaow."

"Now do you believe me?"

"Wait till I catch that blue witch, Greenie. I'll make *her* invisible."

This is another **narrative**. Remember that narratives tell a story. **Speech marks** are placed around the spoken language of Pinkie and Greenie in the story.

**Speech marks** are punctuation marks that are placed around spoken language. They are put at the beginning and at the end of what each person says; for example, **"Come here, Greenie."**

## Let's find them!

These sentences from the text have left their **speech marks** behind. Add them correctly.
For example: "Come here, Greenie," says Pinkie.

Some people use single speech marks 'like this' and some use double marks "like this", but they both work in the same way.

1. What do you want, Pinkie? asks Greenie.

2. I think you stole my black cat, says Pinkie.

3. Shhh. Someone will hear you! whispers Greenie.

4. I don't believe you, Pinkie replies.
5. Miaow, miaow, miaow.
6. Now do you believe me?

## Let's go to the next step!

Add **speech marks** to the sentences below.
For example: "I would like to be Greenie in the play," said Louis.

1. Shhh, the green witch whispered.
2. Ben asked, Is it fun pretending to act on the stage?
3. My parents are coming to see our play tonight, said Koba.
4. Millie asked, Did you hear the audience clapping loudly?
5. Next year I hope I can be in our school play, sighed Joanne.
6. You have got your lines muddled up, said Ashley.

## Let's aim high now!

There are too many **speech marks** in these sentences. Circle those that aren't needed.
For example: Ravi said, "I like plays that have magic in them." They are my favourite."

1. "I hope I can be the cat in the play," said" Tina.
2. "Can I be the giant in the play?" "asked Jack.
3. "He would make a good prince in the play," I said."
4. "Are you the prince" in the play?" I asked.
5. "What does your costume look like?" "she enquired.
6. "That play is really very funny," "said Billie. "It made me laugh out loud."

## The class play

"**Good morning, Year Two,**" said Ms Gibb. "Today we begin work on our class play."

"Can I be in the play?" asked Ben.

"Can I?" called out Hermann.

**Alex added, "Can I be in the play?"**

"Quietly please!" said Ms Gibb firmly. "We will all choose who is best at each part."

"Will there be a part for everyone?" asked Alex.

"There certainly will, Alex. But not everyone can have a main part. There are only four main parts and there are fifteen of you."

Su-Lin asked, "What is the play about?"

"It is about lost treasure and pirates," Ms Gibb said with a smile.

"That sounds good," said Alex.

"I thought you'd like that," said Ms Gibb.

This is another **conversation**. Remember that conversations are **spoken exchanges** between people. This conversation about the class play has been written down; punctuation marks have been used to show the spoken words.

Punctuation marks, including **speech marks**, are used to show how spoken words are said, and when they begin and end. A **comma** is needed to make a pause before an opening speech mark when other words come before it; for example, **Alex added, "Can I be in the play?"**

A punctuation mark, such as a comma, question mark or exclamation mark, is used before a closing speech mark when the sentence is incomplete; for example **"Good morning, Year Two," said Ms Gibb**.

## Let's find them!

These sentences from the text have left their **speech marks** behind.
Add them correctly.
For example: "Can I be in the play?" asked Ben.

1. Can I? called out Hermann.
2. Quietly please! said Ms Gibb firmly.
3. Will there be a part for everyone? asked Alex.

4 Su-Lin asked, What is the play about?

5 That sounds good, said Alex.

6 I thought you'd like that, said Ms Gibb.

## Let's go to the next step!

These sentences have lost the **commas** they need before their **opening speech marks**. Add the commas in the correct places.
For example: Mary asked, "Can I have a main part, please?"

1 Su-Lin whispered "You are on stage in five minutes."

2 Ben said "I am going to be a pirate in our play."

3 Jill asked "Which part are you in our play?"

4 Jimmy shouted "Beware of me. I am a pirate!"

5 Ms Gibb said "We have a song to learn for the play."

6 Icara shouted "Stop her. She's hidden my costume."

## Let's aim high now!

These sentences have lost the **commas** they need before their **closing speech marks**. Add the commas in the correct places.
For example: "Su-Lin got a good part," Hermann said.

1 "I really want to be in the play " Bill called out.

2 "I"m a pirate too " said Alex.

3 "Let's begin our play reading " said the teacher.

4 "You acted that well, Billie " said Mary-Lou.

5 "I'll be so glad when this play is over " moaned George.

6 "I hope we can we have a cast party " giggled Jenny.

## Let's put it together now!

There should be six **opening** and six **closing speech marks** included in the conversation below. Add them in the right places.

Mum, have you seen my costume? asked Ben.

No, Ben, answered his mum. Did you bring it home from school? she asked.

I think so, said Ben.

I saw it in the boot of the car last night, said Ben's dad.

Thank goodness, said Ben.

## Let's have fun!

Sometimes speech bubbles are used instead of speech marks to show what people say. Underline the words inside the speech marks in the text below. Write these words (without their speech marks) into the correct **speech bubbles** and then add the correct punctuation.

"Yowieeeeee!" said the cat.

"Oops, I'm so sorry," said the king.

"You shall be punished!" said the queen.

# Let's have a test!

In questions 1–3, choose the punctuation mark that is missing from the boxes.

1 "Our play is on tonight, [ ] announced Josie.

◯ ! ◯ , ◯ . ◯ "

2 "Gran couldn't come to see our play [ ]" said Antony.

◯ ? ◯ . ◯ , ◯ "

3 Alex asked, [ ] Were you chosen as a pirate in the play?"

◯ " ◯ " ◯ . ◯ ?

In questions 4–5, show where the comma should be.

4 "I'm going to be ◯ a pirate ◯ in the play ◯ " Ben said ◯ happily.

5 Mum ◯ said ◯ "You ◯ acted ◯ well."

In questions 6–7, choose the sentence that has been punctuated correctly.

6
◯ Her father said "It's time to leave"
◯ "It's time to leave." said her father.
◯ "Are you ready to leave?," asked her father.
◯ "Are we leaving now, Dad?" I asked.

7
◯ The actor said "I know my part now."
◯ I learned all my lines, Bill said.
◯ "Do you know your part" asked the teacher.
◯ "Did you learn your lines?" asked Ben.

8 Which sentence has been punctuated **incorrectly**?

◯ "She was a witch in the play." I explained.
◯ "My costume was black and pink," she said.
◯ "I had to miaow like a cat," I said.
◯ "I was invisible in the play," whispered the cat.

# Let's write now!

Write a **conversation** that Pinkie and Greenie have the day after the one in the story called 'Magic tricks'. Take care to use **punctuation marks**, including **speech marks**, correctly.

# Glossary of terms

**Adjectives** describe nouns. They give different kinds of information about the nouns they describe such as number, size, colour, type or an opinion, e.g. six, large, red, outdoor, beautiful.

**Adverbs** add meaning to verbs. They tell how or when something happens, e.g. quickly, today.

**Advertisements** persuade people to do things.

**Commas** (,) are punctuation marks that separate words, or groups of words, in a sentence or in a list.

**Conjunctions** are joining words, e.g. and, but.

**Conversations** are spoken exchanges between people. They can be spoken aloud or they can be written down to report what was said.

**Descriptions** help us form pictures in our mind of people, places and things.

**Diary** entries are personal records written in date order.

**Exclamations** are sentences that express strong feelings such as pleasure, surprise, anger and disgust. They end with an exclamation mark (!).

**Full stops** are punctuation marks shown by a dot (.) at the end of a sentence. They show that the sentence is complete.

**Information reports** give factual information about things, e.g. mammals.

**Letters** are written communications addressed to a person or persons.

**Narratives** tell a story.

**Nouns** are naming words. They can be singular or plural, e.g. boy → boys.

- **Common nouns** name general people, animals, places or things, e.g. girl, dog, country, car.
- **Proper nouns** name specific people, animals, places or things, e.g. Tom, Rover, Australia, Halloween.

**Personal pronouns** are words that are used in place of nouns. They can be singular or plural, e.g. I, we.

**Prepositions** tell us about the position of people, animals, places and things, e.g. on, under, above.

**Prepositional phrases** are groups of words that begin with a preposition and do not have a verb. They can tell when and where, e.g. in the afternoon, at the museum.

**Questions** are sentences that ask for information or opinions. They always end with a question mark (?).

**Recounts** tell about things that have already happened.

**Sentences** are groups of words that make sense on their own. They always start with a capital letter and can end with a full stop, question mark or exclamation mark.

- A **statement** is a sentence that gives information or expresses an opinion.
- A **simple sentence** is a group of words that makes sense by itself. It has only one verb.
- A **compound sentence** is made up of two simple sentences of equal importance, joined by a conjunction.

**Speech marks** are punctuation marks that are placed around spoken language (“ ” or ‘ ’). They are put at the beginning and at the end of what each person says.

**Tense** shows when an action takes place, such as in the **present**, **past** or **future**, e.g. walk (present), walked (past), will walk (future).

**Verbs** are words that show what people, animals or things do. Types of verbs are:

- **being verbs**, e.g. is, was
- **having verbs**, e.g. has, had
- **doing verbs**, e.g. jump, run
- **helping verbs**, e.g. *is* learning, *has* thrown
- **saying verbs**, e.g. said, shouted
- **thinking verbs**, e.g. thinks, wondered.

# Answers

## Unit 1 Wild animals

**Let's find them!** (page 1)

**1** jeep **2** giraffes **3** zebras **4** trail **5** hippos **6** gorillas

**Let's go to the next step!** (page 2)

**2** kangaroo **3** plains **4** cockatoo **5** doctor **6** walrus **7** evening

**Let's aim high now!** (page 2)

| People | Animals | Places | Things |
|---|---|---|---|
| vet | gorillas | plains | food |
| visitor | hippos | waterholes | trees |
| driver | leopards | rivers | ticket |
| zookeeper | bats | parks | bus |
| doctor | cheetahs | grassland | map |
| family | meerkats | forests | hats |
| cleaner | lions | zoos | tails |

**Let's find them!** (page 3)

**1** bamboo **2** water **3** nests **4** trees **5** knuckles **6** feet

**Let's go to the next step!** (page 4)

**2** species **3** forests **4** nests **5** troop **6** tails **7** heads

**Let's aim high now!** (page 4)

**1** lion **2** kangaroo **3** hippo **4** giraffe **5** tiger **6** monkey

**Let's put it together now!** (page 5)

There are gorillas at the zoo who live on an island. They have huge chests and very long arms.
The father has silver fur on his back. He has bright, intelligent eyes. He can hold a stick in his toes.
When the mother wants the children or their father, she claps her hands.

**Let's have a test!** (page 6)

**1** animals **2** vehicle **3** gorillas **4** Giraffes **5** bird **6** zookeeper **7** zoo **8** nest

## Unit 2 People and places

**Let's find them!** (page 7)

**1** Holden **2** *Sealion 2000* **3** Penneshaw **4** Kylie Minogue **5** Akubra **6** Blue Gum

**Let's go to the next step!** (page 8)

**2** Donald Bradman **3** James **4** Mrs Wong **5** Sally **6** Maritime Museum **7** Ford

**Let's aim high now!** (page 8)

**2** November **3** Olympic Games **4** Koala-Lou **5** Luna Park **6** Australia **7** Greece

**Let's find them!** (page 9)

**1** Emperor Qin Shi Huang **2** Mount Fuji **3** Japan **4** Disneyland Park **5** Tomorrowland, Fantasyland, Adventureland **6** Indiana Jones

**Let's go to the next step!** (page 10)

**2** April **3** Disneyland **4** Mickey Mouse **5** Donald Duck **6** Tomorrowland

**Let's aim high now!** (page 10)

You should keep: Father Christmas, Anthony Browne, Vegemite, Anzac Biscuits, Darwin, Tasmania

Incorrect: Sister, Great-Grandfather, Chocolates, Apples, River, Island

**Let's have a test!** (page 12)

**1** Rufus **2** Toyota **3** November **4** canberra **5** mazda **6** Toast **7** You can see Indiana Jones at Adventureland. **8** Jenny saw the Prime Minister in Canberra.

## Unit 3 At the beach

**Let's find them!** (page 13)

**1** glassy, greenish **2** lacy **3** huge **4** green **5** tiny **6** cosy, hot

**Let's go to the next step!** (page 14)

**2** little **3** huge **4** fantastic **5** hot **6** cool **7** yellow

### Let's aim high now! (page 14)

**2** three **3** third **4** giant **5** plastic **6** jagged **7** naughty

### Let's find them! (page 15)

**1** little **2** giant-sized **3** friendly **4** fascinating
**5** delicious **6** two

### Let's go to the next step! (page 16)

**2** clear, blue **3** fantastic **4** 365 **5** salty **6** fishing
**7** good

### Let's aim high now! (page 16)

| Number | Size | Colour | Opinion |
|---|---|---|---|
| first | small | bright | ugly |
| another | tiny | rosy | funny |
| eighty | little | greenish | wonderful |
| last | gigantic | dark | amazing |
| most | huge | red | fantastic |
| few | mini | cream | pretty |

### Let's put it together now! (page 17)

Our holiday house has thirty steps down to the beach. On warm, sunny days I pack my old swimsuit, my favourite, striped towel, sandwiches and a cold drink into my bag. Then I run down the steps and find a good spot on the warm sand.

Sometimes I like to build a huge sandcastle on the beach. My biggest sandcastle had four levels and a wide moat. It was the best sandcastle I've ever made.

### Let's have a test! (page 18)

**1** sunny **2** deep **3** few **4** eight **5** gigantic **6** short
**7** wonderful **8** pretty

## Unit 4 My class

### Let's find them! (page 19–20)

2 The teacher asked me to sit next to Eva Miller.
3 She [Eva] helped me put my things away.
4 Our teacher is called Ms Blewett.
5 I drew Eva and Eva drew me.
6 I can't wait.

### Let's go to the next step! (page 20)

It is time for our camp at last. We leave tomorrow at 7am. I have packed my sleeping bag and some warm clothes. I've got some chocolate milk and fruit scones for morning tea. I hope I can sit next to Bill on the bus. We are going to swim and rock climb. It should be really good.

### Let's aim high now! (page 20)

2 Mike had a new lunchbox. It had stickers on the lid.
3 Ms Blewett is our teacher. She has two children of her own.
4 I like our new classroom. Do you like it?
5 Eva likes ballet. Her sister does too.
6 Our new tables are yellow. Yellow is a happy colour.
7 I did a painting. It is a picture of Eva.

### Let's find them! (page 21)

2 singing, chanting and calling out
3 sleeping bag, pyjamas, toothbrush and toothpaste
4 bats, balls and skipping ropes
5 toast, sausages and eggs
6 rounders, mini-golf, tennis and cricket

### Let's go to the next step! (page 22)

2 We needed paper, pencils and cards to play the game.
3 Would you pass me my t-shirt, book and sweets?
4 They played rugby, soccer and cricket at the camp.
5 The magician found a rabbit, a coin and a feather in my ear!
6 You have to take a sleeping bag, pyjamas and a washbag to camp.
7 We had pears, ice-cream and jelly for dessert.

### Let's aim high now! (page 22)

**2** , white **3** , ice-cream **4** , books **5** , danced
**6** , jeans **7** , dry

### Let's put it together now (page 23)

Bakery: raisin bread, bread rolls, sliced bread
Bathroom items: band aids, bandages, shampoo, toilet rolls
Fruit and vegetables: lettuce, tomatoes, bananas, watermelon, apples
Groceries: tomato sauce, cheese, Vegemite, milk, eggs
Meat: lamb chops, minced steak, sausages

### Let's have fun! (page 23)

Box 1a—Eva has two things for morning tea—chocolate milk and fruit.
Box 1b—Eva has three things for morning tea—chocolate, milk and fruit.
Box 2a—Lochie is putting three items in his bag—an orange, a drink bottle and his beach towel.

Box 2b—Lochie is putting two items in his bag—an orange drink bottle and his beach towel.

**Let's have a test!** (page 24)

**1** [ . ] **2** [ . ] **3** [ . Afterwards] **4** [ , lit ]
**5** [ , raincoats] **6** [ , books] **7** [ , teddy ]
**8** [ , uniform]

## Unit 5 At school

**Let's find them!** (page 25–26)

1 "How old are you, Sam?"
2 "What sports do you like?"
3 "Do you have Aussie Rules here in Sydney?"
4 "Have you heard of them?"
5 "Where should I put my bag?"

**Let's go to the next step!** (page 26)

**2** [ ? ] **3** [ . ] **4** [ . ] **5** [ ? ] **6** [ ? ] **7** [ . ]

**Let's aim high now!** (page 26)

3 Ms Raye lost her old briefcase.
4 Lunchtime begins at 12.30.
6 We have choir after school.
7 No. My school uniform is far too big for me.
5 Our first camp is in Year Three.
2 Next year we will have a new teacher.

**Let's find them!** (page 27)

1 Preston was in the lead!
2 The judges said it was almost a dead heat!
3 It was Preston!
4 Hooray!

**Let's go to the next step!** (page 28)

1 Harry walks to school each day.
2 It is fifteen kilometres to Harry's school. He walks there and back every day!
3 The school canteen sells salad, rolls and fruit for our lunches.
4 I can have a sleepover. Yippee!
5 That's horrible. Yuk!
6 Our school play this year is *Mary Poppins*.

**Let's aim high now!** (page 28)

**2** ? **3** ! **4** . **5** ? **6** ? **7** !

**Let's put it together now!** (page 29)

I am starting at my new school tomorrow. Lizzy who lives next door has said I can walk with her to school. She will show me where everything is. She said she would introduce me to her friends as well. I have a new schoolbag and a new uniform to wear tomorrow. It is green check. I've also got new white socks and a new lunch box. But even so, I'm scared stiff!
*by Tina*

**Let's have a test!** (page 30)

**1** What time does school start? **2** Is there football practice today. **3** How old is your school.
**4** Help! **5** ? **6** ! **7** The rubbish bins look disgusting.
**8** What a disaster.

## Unit 6 Neighbours

**Let's find them!** (page 31–32)

**1** They **2** them **3** it **4** we **5** he **6** she

**Let's go to the next step!** (page 32)

**1** she **2** it **3** we **4** he **5** she **6** it

**Let's aim high now!** (page 32)

**1** his, Jim **2** she, Molly **3** they, Coopers
**4** her, Susan **5** it, house **6** you, Anna

**Let's find them!** (page 33)

**1** it **2** It **3** he **4** We **5** them **6** they

**Let's go to the next step!** (page 34)

**1** singular **2** plural, singular **3** singular, plural
**4** singular **5** plural **6** singular, singular

**Let's aim high now!** (page 34)

**2** he **3** she **4** them **5** we **6** they **7** I

**Let's put it together now!** (page 35)

The neighbours from next door have six children. [They] also have a dog, a cat, chickens, guinea pigs and a turtle. Jenny and [I] like visiting so [we] can see all the animals. Mrs Snow lets [me] feed the dog and cat. [She] said [I] could get the eggs from the chickens when [I] am a bit older. Mrs Snow's eldest son is allowed to get the eggs as [he] is ten. Jenny likes watching the guinea pigs. [She] feeds [them] grass. The turtle moves around very slowly. [It] isn't afraid of [us] though. [We] love having such interesting neighbours as [they] keep [us] busy!

**Let's have fun** (page 35)

1  John has cooked a cake and it has lots of icing.
2  Would you give me a turn on the skateboard, please?
3  She piled muffins on a plate for the visitors.

4  They ran fast to catch the school bus.

5  Wow! Is that a present for me?

**Let's have a test!** (page 36)

**1** her, his, you, I **2** he **3** it **4** she **5** them **6** them **7** she **8** Do you live next door to Bill?

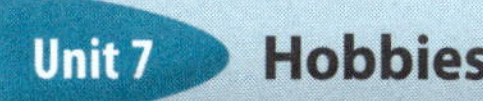

## Unit 7 Hobbies

**Let's find them!** (page 37–38)

**1** swung **2** hit **3** ran or run **4** dropped **5** flew **6** caught

**Let's go to the next step!** (page 38)

**2** toss **3** wobble **4** float **5** look **6** carry **7** wait

**Let's aim high now!** (page 38)

**2** threw, caught **3** swung, missed **4** ran **5** fidget, wriggle **6** climbed, watched **7** come

**Let's find them!** (page 39)

**1** forget **2** remember **3** wonder **4** doubt **5** prefer **6** knew

**Let's go to the next step** (page 40)

**1** hope **2** decide **3** doubt **4** suppose **5** believe **6** imagine

**Let's aim high now!** (page 40)

**2** know **3** forgot **4** realise **5** imagine **6** remember **7** decided

**Let's put it together now!** (page 41)

Head—think, know, wonder
Eyes—see, watch, look
Arms and hands—draw, pat, stroke
Legs and feet—hop, kick, jump
Body—turn, stretch, bend

**Let's have fun!** (page 41)

| Across | Down |
|---|---|
| **3** collect | **1** ski |
| **5** knit | **2** kicks |
| **7** read | **3** cook |
| **8** sing | **4** play |
| **9** make | **6** juggle |

**Let's have a test!** (page 42)

**1** cook, jump, eat, kick **2** paste **3** throw **4** build **5** skated **6** know **7** I hope so. **8** Have you decided whether you will come to the game?

## Unit 8 At the farm

**Let's find them!** (page 43–44)

1 Sometimes I feed them vegetable scraps.
2 We mostly have sheep on our farm.
3 It keeps them safe from foxes.
4 Dad gets up at 5 am.
5 He will buy a tractor soon.

**Let's go to the next step!** (page 44)

**2** fed **3** chirped **4** paddled **5** sold **6** chased **7** moo

**Let's aim high now!** (page 44)

2 Sally owns a pet duck.
3 The ducklings swam with their mother.
4 Tom milks the cows.
5 We swim in the river.
6 The dogs raced across the paddock.
7 I grew a cabbage in our garden.

**Let's find them!** (page 45)

2 Ducks have waterproof feathers and ducks' feet never get cold.
3 Most ducks make a quacking noise but not all ducks quack.
4 Female ducks lay eggs and they keep them warm.
5 Ducklings grow feathers quickly and fly at about 2 months old.

**Let's go to the next step!** (page 46)

**1** (but) **2** (as) **3** (but) **4** (or) **5** (and) **6** (but)

**Let's aim high now!** (page 46)

| First part | Second part |
|---|---|
| Pigs have long snouts | and they have curly tails. |
| This little piggy went to market | but this little piggy stayed home. |
| It has been very dry | so we need plenty of rain. |
| We dug big holes in the soil | and we planted some fruit trees. |
| They picked the fruit | and sold it at the market. |
| The rain fell for seven days | and the dam soon filled. |

**Let's put it together now** (page 47)

My grandparents came to visit our farm **and** I felt very excited. They had a long journey **so** they were tired. The next day we walked around the farm together **and** I showed them the animals. Pa wore his gumboots **and** he wore a woolly scarf around his neck. Gran had warm gloves **and** she wore a thick coat. We couldn't find our cat, Milly, **but** we saw our rooster and the chickens. Gran liked the baby lambs best **but** Pa liked the ducklings. That evening Mum lit a fire **and** Dad lit the lamp. Gran made muffins **and** I made hot chocolate. The room felt cosy **and** we were all as warm as toast.

**Let's have a test!** (page 48)

**1** and **2** but **3** or **4** The cows mooed loudly. **5** The goat chewed my cardboard box. **6** Georgie looks after the hens and she collects the eggs. **7** The fox sniffed at the gate and pushed his nose under it. **8** but

## Unit 9 Recycling

**Let's find them!** (page 49)

**1** present **2** present **3** past **4** past **5** present **6** present **7** past

**Let's go to the next step!** (page 50)

**1** wanted **2** saw **3** helped **4** used **5** saved **6** filled

**Let's aim high now!** (page 50)

| Verb | Tense |
|---|---|
| **2** ate | past |
| **3** used | past |
| **4** has | present |
| **5** contain | present |
| **6** feels | present |
| **7** learned | past |

**Let's find them!** (page 51)

**2** was, past **3** has, past **4** is, present **5** were, past **6** are, present **7** are, present

**Let's go to the next step!** (page 52)

**2** is **3** had **4** am **5** did **6** were **7** was

**Let's aim high now!** (page 52)

| Verb group | Tense |
|---|---|
| **2** had collected | past |
| **3** are harming | present |
| **4** is trying | present |
| **5** were adding | past |
| **6** is going | present |
| **7** was putting | past |

**Let's put it together now!** (page 53)

What am I?

Mel **did** his homework on me. The next day Mel **took** me to school. His teacher **told** him to show me to her. She **looked** at me and then **said** to Mel, "Very good." Mel **put** me in his desk.

At the end of the year, Mel **cleared** out his desk. He **decided** to throw me away. His teacher **told** him to put me in the recycle bin. Hurrah. I **was going** to be made new again.

Answer: I am a piece of paper.

**Let's have fun!** (page 53)

1. Earth hour was begun in Sydney but is now in 135 countries.
2. Have you seen our Earth Hour logo?
3. To save electricity we have used candles tonight.
4. I am going to make a scarecrow at my Earth Hour workshop.

**Let's have a test!** (page 54)

**1** save **2** worked **3** thought **4** think **5** wanted **6** was **7** are **8** had

## Unit 10 Aboriginal culture

**Let's find them!** (page 55)

**1** asked **2** sighed **3** whispered **4** said **5** suggested **6** shouted

**Let's go to the next step!** (page 56)

**1** asked **2** told **3** whispered **4** argue **5** promised **6** explained

**Let's aim high now!** (page 56)

**2** said **3** groaned **4** asked **5** described **6** pleaded **7** announced

**Let's find them!** (page 57)

**2** are **3** is **4** were **5** are **6** have **7** are

**Let's go to the next step!** (page 58)

**1** is **2** is **3** was **4** were **5** is **6** am

**Let's aim high now!** (page 58)

**2** have **3** was **4** has **5** is **6** Were **7** are

### Let's put it together now! (page 59)

| Saying verbs | Being verbs | Having verbs |
|---|---|---|
| **2** explained | **2** was | **2** had |
| **3** said | **3** is | **3** had |
| **4** told | **4** is | |
| **5** repeated | | |

### Let's have fun! (page 59)

| Across | Down |
|---|---|
| **2** was | **1** asks |
| **3** shout | **2** whispered |
| **4** has | **5** are |
| **7** promised | **6** am |
| **8** had | |

### Let's have a test! (page 60)

**1** told **2** She asked where the river began. **3** announced **4** is **5** The didgeridoo was very old. **6** are **7** had **8** The Rainbow Serpent has beautiful colours.

## Unit 11 Story time

### Let's find them! (page 61)

**1** slowly **2** hard **3** still **4** loudly **5** fast **6** luckily

### Let's go to the next step! (page 62)

**2** quietly **3** slowly **4** sadly **5** quickly **6** closely **7** loudly

### Let's aim high now! (page 62)

**1** sat, comfortably **2** ran, swiftly
**3** spoke, crossly **4** stared, angrily
**5** laughed, merrily **6** fell, accidentally

### Let's find them! (page 63)

**1** real **2** proudly **3** then **4** finally **5** nastily **6** cleverly

### Let's go to the next step! (page 64)

| Adverb | How or when? |
|---|---|
| **2** soon | when |
| **3** hungrily | how |
| **4** Afterwards | when |
| **5** hard | how |
| **6** already | when |
| **7** Suddenly | when |

### Let's aim high now! (page 64)

| Adverb | How or when? |
|---|---|
| **2** hurriedly | how |
| **3** violently | how |
| **4** quietly | how |
| **5** often | when |
| **6** properly | how |
| **7** now | when |

### Let's put it together now! (page 65)

"Who has **greedily** eaten my carrots?" she asked.
No answer from her babies.
"Who has stolen my carrots?" she asked **again**.
"Not me," the timid baby rabbit said **shyly**.
"Not me," the brave baby rabbit answered **boldly**.
The mother stared **suspiciously** at them. **Next** she asked, "Where are the twins?"
The baby rabbits **slyly** stole a look at each other. They knew where the twins were hiding! But they were not going to tell.

### Let's have fun! (page 65)

**1** He sneered cruelly.

**2** I am running late.

**3** You yawned rudely.

**4** She slept soundly.

**5** They danced joyfully.

### Let's have a test! (page 66)

**1** I read the story aloud. **2** Jack climbed the beanstalk quickly. **3** She woke from here sleep today! **4** The plane took off immediately. **5** now **6** The pea was secretly hidden under the princess's mattresses. **7** The Rainbow Serpent slid smoothly across the hillside. **8** Charlotte the spider cleverly rescued Wilbur the pig.

## Unit 12 Pets

### Let's find them! (page 67–68)

1 Dogs and cats are very popular pets.
2 Children like to have their own pets.
3 Each pet has different needs.
4 Kittens like to play with toys.
5 Pets need care.

**Let's go to the next step!** (page 68)
**2** lead **3** fed **4** nibble **5** me **6** babies **7** dog

**Let's aim high now!** (page 68)
1 not a statement
2 not a statement
3 statement
4 not a statement
5 statement
6 not a statement

**Let's find them!** (page 69–70)
1 Kittens need their mother's milk to grow strong.
2 She tried to catch her tail.
3 She made my family laugh.
4 I filled her bowl with milk.
5 I think she will learn to use it quickly.

**Let's go to the next step!** (page 70)
**1** fact **2** opinion **3** opinion **4** fact **5** opinion **6** fact

**Let's aim high now!** (page 70)
2 view—opinion
3 think—opinion
4 need—fact
5 beautiful—opinion
6 tail—fact
7 anything—opinion

**Let's put it together now!** (page 71)

| Blue for factual statements | Green for statements of opinion |
|---|---|
| **1** Guinea pigs have hairy coats.<br>**2** Guinea pigs don't have tails.<br>**3** Rabbits live in burrows.<br>**4** Rabbits have long ears.<br>**5** Goldfish have gills.<br>**6** Goldfish live in freshwater. | **1** I think my guinea pig might bite me.<br>**2** Guinea pigs are kind.<br>**3** Rabbits are always friendly.<br>**4** Rabbits make most people sneeze.<br>**5** In my view goldfish should all be set free.<br>**6** Goldfish are very smart animals. |

**Let's have a test!** (page 72)
**1** The goldfish is in her bowl. **2** I hope you won't wake my kitten. **3** Very young kittens drink milk from their mothers. **4** Horses have four legs. **5** Some birds are kept in cages. **6** Rabbits make the best pets in the world. **7** It is unkind to keep birds in cages. **8** People look after their pets very well in my view.

## Unit 13 Museums

**Let's find them!** (page 73)
**2** on **3** around **4** of **5** on **6** inside **7** into **8** from **9** in **10** on

**Let's go to the next step!** (page 74)
**2** at **3** beside **4** from **5** in **6** to **7** until

**Let's aim high now!** (page 74)
**1** above **2** across **3** near **4** along **5** by **6** beside

**Let's find them!** (page 75–76)
1 next month
2 from the past
3 in the entrance
4 in the other rooms
5 on the wall
6 in a few days

**Let's go to the next step!** (page 76)
**2** next to **3** on **4** with **5** in **6** inside **7** at

**Let's aim high now!** (page 76)
**1** when **2** where **3** where **4** when **5** where **6** when

**Let's have fun** (page 77)
There are twelve prepositional phrases in the instructions:
Come **out of the motel** and turn **to the right**. Walk **along the path**, **over the hill** and **across the road**. Go **up the steps**, **into the museum** and **past the counter**. Go **through the doorway** and turn **to the right**. Go **in the second door** and you will be **in the room** that has the old toys.

**Let's have a test!** (page 78)
**1** She paid for her ticket at the window. **2** beside **3** across **4** over **5** The Space Museum is in Washington. **6** Museums have websites on the Internet. **7** The National Museum has guided tours on Sundays. **8** The Golden Dragon Museum opens everyday.

## Unit 14 On the stage

### Let's find them! (page 79–80)

1 “What do you want, Pinkie?” asks Greenie.
2 “I think you stole my black cat,” says Pinkie.
3 “Shhh. Someone will hear you!” whispers Greenie.
4 “I don't believe you,” Pinkie replies.
5 “Miaow, miaow, miaow.”
6 “Now do you believe me?”

### Let's go to the next step! (page 80)

1 “Shhh,” the green witch whispered.
2 Ben asked, “Is it fun pretending to act on the stage?”
3 “My parents are coming to see our play tonight,” said Koba.
4 Millie asked, “Did you hear the audience clapping loudly?”
5 “Next year I hope I can be in our school play,” sighed Joanne.
6 “You have got your lines muddled up,” said Ashley.

### Let's aim high now! (page 80)

1 “I hope I can be the cat in the play,” said” Tina.
2 “Can I be the giant in the play?” “asked Jack.
3 “He would make a good prince in the play,” I said.”
4 “Are you the prince” in the play?” I asked.
5 “What does your costume look like?” “she enquired.
6 “That play is really very funny,” “said Billie. “It made me laugh out loud.”

### Let's find them! (page 81–82)

1 “Can I?” called out Hermann.
2 “Quietly please!” said Ms Gibb firmly.
3 “Will there be a part for everyone?” asked Alex.
4 Su-Lin asked, “What is the play about?”
5 “That sounds good,” said Alex.
6 “I thought you'd like that,” said Ms Gibb.

### Let's go to the next step! (page 82)

1 Su-Lin whispered, “You are on stage in five minutes.”
2 Ben said, “I am going to be a pirate in our play.”
3 Jill asked, “Which part are you in our play?”
4 Jimmy shouted, “Beware of me. I am a pirate!”
5 Ms Gibb said, “We have a song to learn for the play.”
6 Icara shouted, “Stop her. She's hidden my costume.”

### Let's aim high now! (page 82)

1 “I really want to be in the play,” Bill called out.
2 “I'm a pirate too,” said Alex.
3 “Let's begin our play reading,” said the teacher.
4 “You acted well, Billie,” said Mary-Lou.
5 “I'll be so glad when this play is over,” moaned George.
6 “I hope we can we have a cast party,” giggled Jenny.

### Let's put it together now! (page 83)

“Mum, have you seen my costume?” asked Ben.
“No, Ben,” answered his mum. “Did you bring it home from school?” she asked.
“I think so,” said Ben.
“I saw it in the boot of the car last night,” said Ben's dad.
“Thank goodness,” said Ben.

### Let's have fun (page 83)

**1** Yowieeee! **2** Oops, I'm so sorry. **3** You shall be punished!

### Let's have a test! (page 84)

**1** ” **2** , **3** “ **4** play,” **5** said, “ **6** “Are we leaving now, Dad?” I asked. **7** “Did you learn your lines?” asked Ben. **8** “She was a witch in the play,” I explained.

# Notes